The Seaside

The Seaside
Sarah Howell

Author's Note

I should like to thank all the many people who have helped in
the preparation of this book, particularly those who very kindly
lent me their precious photographs, postcards, books and
souvenirs for the illustrations, including Miss Amy Bailey,
Miss Barbara Jones, Miss Margaret Gray, Mrs Beryl Vosburgh,
Mr Michael Davies, Mr Lionel Lambourne, and especially
Mr Robert Scott. I must also thank Mr H. Beresford-Bourke
for his advice on the section on Edwardian postcards, Mr A. E.
Collins for his information on the elusive history of seaside
rock, and the staff of the Wolverhampton Art Gallery for all their
help in locating souvenirs. I am also very grateful to Michael
Sossick and Nick Jacobsen for taking photographs for me and to
Mick Keniger for kindly lending me his thesis and photographs.
It would be impossible to list all the friends who have helped
me with ideas and information, but I am especially grateful to
Michael Blaker, my sister Jessica York, my mother, and to my
husband who had the idea in the first place.

Title page illustration Photograph by Paul Martin

Studio Vista
Cassell & Collier Macmillan Publishers Limited, London
35 Red Lion Square, London WC1R 4SG

© 1974 Sarah Howell
Designed by Marie-Louise Luxemburg

Set in 11 on 12 pt Imprint
Filmset and printed Offset Litho by
Cox & Wyman Ltd,
London, Fakenham and Reading
ISBN 0 289 70311 5

Contents

Detail from *View of Scarborough* by John Setterington, 1735

~ House | B. *Hall* B. *A* | C. *The Long Room* | D. *Blands Cliff Road* | To the Hon.ᵇˡᵉ JOHN HILL Esq. one of
~d *Gd* | F. *The Post House* | G. *East Sand Gate* | H. *The Town Hall* | This PERSPECTIVE Draught of the ANTIENT T
is humbly dedicated by his most Obliged and Devoted

The New Watering-Places

It was in England, early in the eighteenth century, that people first began to visit decaying ports and small fishing villages in order to bathe by the sea. Before then sea-bathing was almost unheard of in Europe; it was resorted to only as a desperate and ineffective cure for the bite of a mad dog. Even the maritime English, whose wealth and safety depended on it, left the sea to sailors and fishermen.

Swimming was looked upon not as a pleasant pastime or a sport, but only as a useful military accomplishment – 'a great helpe in the extreamitie of death', wrote the author of a sixteenth-century treatise *De Arte Natandi*. Boys must sometimes have been unable to resist the temptation to splash about in rivers or ponds on hot summer days, but the most innocent bathing, if it was done solely for pleasure, often met with stern moral disapproval. In 1571 the Vice-Chancellor of Cambridge issued a decree forbidding members of the university to bathe in the Cam. The penalty for undergraduates was a public flogging, for Bachelors of Arts a spell in the stocks. This harsh attitude is difficult to explain. The classically educated ruling classes seem to have associated bathing with the orgies of ancient Rome, and perhaps they half-expected wanton, tempting nymphs to rise up out of the water. Towards the end of the seventeenth century this prejudice did begin to lessen. Bathing in pools and rivers became quite common, but the sea was still ignored.

Doctors first made sea-bathing respectable; and the idea that the seaside is good for you has been part of our folklore ever since. Resorts have always encouraged this feeling, emphasizing different health-giving qualities to fit in with medical fashion. Sea-bathing, sea-water drinking, the sea air, the ozone, and the sunshine have followed each other as seaside panaceas, even the east wind does you good in Skegness – it is 'so bracing'.

For almost a hundred years after they first tentatively took the plunge, the English were the only people in Europe who bathed in the sea; and seaside resorts were thriving and fashionable in England long before they began to exist on the Continent. Even in the eighteenth century, few parts of England were more than three or four days' journey from the coast, but the early rise of the seaside resorts was probably due less to geography or to the theories of a few medical men, than to the unique role which the spas played in upper-class English life.

The spas were ancient and adaptable institutions. They had taken their name in the sixteenth century from the town of Spa in Belgium, but their history goes far back into antiquity. Bath and Buxton and several hot springs on the Continent had been used by the Romans, and many spas were places of pilgrimage in the Middle Ages. Baden, Spa and Vichy flourished in the sixteenth and early seventeenth centuries, but in England it was not until the Restoration that the great age of the spas began. Charles II's queen came to Tunbridge Wells hoping to find a cure for her barrenness. The waters seem to have had the desired effect on many court ladies, though not on poor Catherine, but more crucial for Tunbridge and the other spas was the way her stay there transformed the atmosphere of the place. Courtiers amused themselves with intrigues, gambling, open-air dancing and bowls, and soon other visitors began to follow their example. By the end of the seventeenth century the three most important spas in England, Tunbridge Wells, Epsom and Bath were 'more famed for pleasure than cures'. From this period the English spas seem to have been much more genial than their continental models. French observers noted with surprise that if the people who visited them had illnesses, they were certainly not of a kind to interfere with their enjoyment.

In the late seventeenth and early eighteenth centuries hundreds of new spas were developed in England, either from old holy wells or from newly discovered springs. There was an extraordinary number of mineral springs in London, and round them grew up theatres, gardens, and public rooms for dancing. Places like Islington, Streatham, Bagnigge Wells – the favourite haunt of city tradesmen – and Sadler's Wells were famous London spas, but there were scores of others. By the mid-eighteenth century it seemed as if no area on the outskirts of the city could succeed in attracting people for recreation unless it had a spa. Both Hampstead and Richmond fortunately discovered them.

It was Bath that set the pattern for all the English spas outside London, and made them so important in the social and cultural life of the country. Richard Nash, who became Master of Ceremonies there in 1705, changed it from a disorderly town full of gamblers into the most fashionable place in the kingdom. He succeeded in making Bath irresistible to the nobility, and he had such total self-assurance that they were prepared to accept his rigid rules with scarcely a murmur. He banned all private entertainments and insisted that even the grandest duchess should be civil to anyone he chose to accept. To people on the fringes of the aristocracy – country squires, parsons and rich merchants – Bath became the best place to learn urbanity and meet the right people, a sort of vast finishing school.

Elegant assembly rooms, pump-rooms, circulating libraries and theatres were built in imitation of Bath by other English spas like Buxton, Tunbridge Wells and Harrogate. They acquired Masters of Ceremonies to organize and preside over social life and they also 'trod upon the heels of Bath in gaiety and dissipation'.

In spite of all the pleasant distractions, the healing powers of spa waters were taken seriously. They brought hope of a cure to invalids and hypochondriacs at a time when most other medical treatment was primitive and painful, and there grew up a whole literature in exaggerated praise of the properties of the mineral springs. It was this medical propaganda that brought the first glimmers of public interest in sea-water. At the end of the seventeenth century some doctors, often those who practised at spas which did not boast hot springs, began to discover curative properties in cold-water bathing, and this in turn led to the first suggestions that bathing in the sea might be beneficial. Sir John Floyer, a physician with connections in Buxton, recommended frequent cold baths for vigour, strength and hardiness. He considered that hot springs, like those at Bath, 'corrupted manners and made bodies effeminate'. In the *History of Cold Bathing* he became really eloquent about the virtues of sea-water. 'Since we live on an island and have the Sea about us, we cannot want an excellent Cold Bath which will preserve our Healths and cure many Diseases, as our Fountains do.' His list of ills it could cure was as wild and diverse as any of the contemporary claims that were being made for spa waters. It included leprosy, cancer, gonorrhoea, deafness and corns. He even suddenly burst into rhyme.

> Cold bathing has this good alone;
> It makes old John to hug old Joan!
> And does fresh kindnesses entail,
> On a wife, tasteless, old and stale.

Even before Sir John Floyer had discovered all these new virtues in sea-water, a Dr Wittie had suggested in the

1660s that the sea 'cured gout', 'dried up superfluous humours' and 'killed all manner of worms'. He had made these claims in a book called *Scarborough Spaw* which was principally concerned with listing the merits of the mineral spring at Scarborough; and as the town was on the coast, he had thrown in the therapeutic powers of the sea as an additional attraction.

Seventy years later, as Dr Wittie had prophesied, the sea did begin to give Scarborough a unique edge over other spas. Its medicinal spring had been discovered under the cliffs early in the seventeenth century, but when Celia Fiennes (the record of whose travels was published in the 1880s as *Through England on a Side-Saddle in the Time of William and Mary*) visited Yorkshire in 1679, Scarborough was, in spite of its ancient castle and fine harbour, a dull little town: 'all the diversion is ye walking on this sand twice a day at ye ebb of the tide.' By the 1730s, its atmosphere had changed and it had become the most fashionable spa in the north. 'These waters fraught with virtues formerly known to few and healing chiefly the sick of inferior rank .'. . now cheer the spirits, and brace the nerves of peers as well as commoners.' The waters were not the only attraction. It is obvious from contemporary descriptions that by the 1730s sea-bathing was an essential part of the life of visitors to the town, and must have been one of the main reasons why they went there. Thus Scarborough, a spa that happened to be by the sea, became the very first seaside resort.

A book published in 1734, *The Letters of a Gentleman from Scarborough*, though it reads like an early exercise in public relations, gives an interesting picture of life in the town. The anonymous author is far more interested in describing the bathing arrangements than in tediously reiterating the properties of the spa. 'The gentlemen go out a little way to sea in boats and jump in naked directly. There are two little houses on the shore to retire to for dressing in.' The ladies, he says, 'have the use of gowns and guides'. There is a famous engraving by Setterington printed in the following year which complements this description. One half of it shows Scarborough Castle dominating the harbour with sailing boats. riding at anchor, and the other is a view of the beach. Setterington looked at the scene with a clear, objective eye. There is none of the broad comedy or satire with which later in the eighteenth century graphic artists loaded similar scenes. His little figures swim and gambol about quite naked – revealing, as well as everything else, their vulnerable cropped heads, for they would not have wanted to get their wigs wet. The bathers are drawn as elegantly as the gentlemen on horseback on the sands, the sedan-chairs, and the ladies holding hands on the water's edge. Setterington shows the boats mentioned in the *Letters of a Gentleman* – from which the men bathed – though not the huts on the shore for dressing and undressing. The boats seem to have died out soon after this time, for there is no mention or drawing of them later in the century. He also shows the first recorded bathing-machine. It is the little pavilion with four wheels and a pointed roof parked at the water's edge. A naked gentleman is descending from it into the waves while the door is held open for him by a liveried servant. Perhaps the machine was a private one, for there are no others on the beach. It was certainly a portent. For almost 200 years, bathing-machines, scarcely changed in their essentials, were to be an inescapable feature of every English seaside resort. They became the subject of innumerable jokes and cartoons, complaints and by-laws – the cumbersome, comic symbols of the English seaside until the First World War.

The whole atmosphere of Setterington's print is unself-conscious and innocent, but the streak of wild vulgarity which runs through the history of seaside resorts like the pink letters in their rock was present at their very beginning. Dicky Dickinson, the first Governor of Scarborough Spaw, was seaside rudery personified. He rented the mineral water spring from the corporation and built 'two houses of conveniency, one for the use of gentlemen, the other for ladies. The custom is as soon as you enter the room to subscribe your name in Dicky's book and pay five shillings after which you may have free use of his retirements.'

Purging was an essential part of the treatment at spas in those days of gross over-eating, and the waters at Scarborough were, as Celia Fiennes had noted, particularly effective in this respect. This fact and Dicky's jokes on the subject were considered an attraction by the people who stayed in the town in the early eighteenth century.

> Yet shall my Dicky's favrite name,
> Shine foremost in the list of Fame.
> I'll make him Sovreign of the Spaw
> To keep the Squirting Tribe in awe,
> The Loosest shall obey his Law,
> Nor shall he ever want a Wile
> To make Fools laugh or Ladies smile.
> His face shall be so like a Fool
> His very looks shall give a stool.

It was only rarely that fastidious visitors were put off, though when Sarah Duchess of Marlborough visited Scarborough in 1732 she left as quickly as she could in case she might have to use Dicky's 'retirements'.

Mr RICHARD DICKINSON of SCARBOROUGH SPAW.

A Mighty MONARCH here I Reign,   For you muſt know, that very morn,
And Lord it over Land and Main;   When I by Fate's decree was born,
Both Sea and Land their Tribute bring,   The God of Phyſick great APOLLO
And both conſpire to prove me KING: Beſpoke th'aſſembled Gods as follows:
The Sea it ſelf does twice a day   This wondrous Infant ſhall not riſe
Advance, and Homage to me pay;   From Arms or Politicks his Pra
Yet ſome infer (like Sons of Wh–s)   No Crown or Scepter, no, nor Mace
NEPTUNE grown jealous of our Powers   His head or hand ſhall ever grace;
Turns Me and PEGGY out of doors;   Yet ſhall my DICKY's favrit' name
Becauſe he once or twice a year   Shine foremoſt in the liſt of Fame
Within my Palace dare appear: I'll make him SOV'REIGN of the SPAW,
Whereas the good old God prepares   To keep the Squirting Tribe in awe,
Only to waſh my Hall and Stairs: The LOOSEST ſhall obey his Law.
Others (who love a modiſh Wh–re,   Nor ſhall he ever want a Wiſe
Or as they call it an Amour,   To make Fools laugh and Ladies ſmile;
That ſo their great Examples may   His face ſhall be ſo like a Fool,
Excuſe their faults) are apt to ſay,   His very looks ſhall give a ſtool:
That I and PEGGY oft have done,   And leaſt his Poſtures ſhould in fact
As LEWIS GRAND with MAINTENON: A looſneſs from the SPAW contract,
But grant, ſuppoſe that this is true;   And it ſhould give him too much trouble.
I aſk, what's it Sirs, to you: His ſhape like SCARONS ſhall be double.
I rule with Univerſal Sway,   Reſembling much the letter Z,
WHIGS, TORIES, JACKS me Tribute pay;   But (wit aſide) not quite ſo bad,
And when their Taxes I receive,   In ſhort he ſhall not walk upright,
Lord, how I laugh within my ſleeve!   But in a poſture fit to ſh–te.
Nor do I rack my brain t'indite
Force'd complements, but ſay, Go ſh–te,
Or elſe I ſneer and cry, A Bite.

* Dicky's lovely Handmaid

Dicky Dickinson, the
first Governor of
Scarborough Spaw,
from *The Letters of a
Gentleman from
Scarborough*, 1734

As well as drinking the waters, purging and bathing, there were other robust amusements. At low tide one rode on the sands. 'The recess of the sea leaves a beautiful parterre upon the sands, of two miles, the whole as level as a bowling green, and at that time all sorts of sprightly exercises and genteel diversions go forward there; particularly horseracing, frequent at the season, either for plate given by the town, or by contribution of the company.' There were sedan-chairs if it rained, travelling players to be watched in the afternoons, a coffee-house and bookseller and huge meals to look forward to.

In the evenings people went to the Long Room built overlooking the sea. 'Here are balls every evening, when the room is illuminated like a court assembly . . . Gentlemen (only) pay for dancing one shilling each; on one side of the room is a music gallery, and at the lower end are kept a pharo bank, a hazard table and fair chance; and in the side-rooms tables for such of the company as are inclined to play at cards; below stairs you have billiard tables. It is kept by Mr. Vipont, master of the Long Room at Hampstead . . . the house is provided with cooks from London.' By the 1730s London tradesmen, sedan-chair men and upholsterers, as well as cooks, found it worth their while to set up branches of their businesses at Scarborough, and Mr Vipont must have been one of the first of the many inland spa officials who were later to migrate to the seaside.

Scarborough was the only really flourishing sea-bathing place in the period from 1730 to 1750, but other coastal towns were just beginning to attract visitors. Bathing brought a few invalids to towns like Eastbourne, Deal, Portsmouth and Exmouth and there is an interesting letter from the Rev William Clarke describing a holiday he spent at Brighton, then called Brighthelmstone, in 1736. It was at that time still only a run-down fishing port, but a packet-boat service to Dieppe had just been started, and its days of fame and fashion were not far off. 'We are now sunning ourselves on the beach at Brighthelmstone. . . . Such a tract of sea; such regions of corn. . . . But the mischief is, that we have little conversation besides the *clamor nauticus*. . . . My morning business is bathing in the sea, and then buying fish; the evening is riding out for air, viewing the remains of old Saxon camps, and counting the ships in the road and the boats that are trawling. . . . The lodgings are as *low* as they are cheap; we have two parlours, *two bed chambers, pantry etc.* for five shillings a week; and if you will really come down you need not fear a bed of the proper dimensions.'

The man most responsible for the transformation of Brighton and the seaside mania of the second half of the eighteenth century was Dr Richard Russell. In 1750 he published the *Dissertation on the Use of Seawater in Diseases of the Glands*. Like many people who seem to start a fashion, Dr Russell was not, in fact, very original. He developed ideas and trends that were already in the air and his work appeared at just the right moment. Bath was then still in its prime, and the pattern of spa life had been set, but Beau Nash was nearly eighty and his rule was almost over. Bath and the other spas had long years of high fashion ahead of them, but by 1750 many genuine invalids must have realized that spa waters could do little for their particular diseases, and many pleasure seekers must have been ready for some slightly different diversions.

The Latin first edition of Russell's *Dissertation* was followed later in the 1750s by five editions of a pirated English version, as well as a translation by Dr Russell himself. It was eagerly bought by the general public and long remained a favourite in circulating libraries. (Mrs Thrale describes a man who came hopping into Bowen's library in Brighton in 1780 asking for 'Russell on Sea Water'.) It is difficult now to understand this great popularity, but at that time new reading matter was scarce, except for sermons, and perhaps some people ploughed through it out of morbid curiosity, for Russell describes in much detail the gruesome symptoms of his 'elegant cases'. When, in the nineteenth century, France caught up with the English fashion for sea-bathing, his book became popular on the Continent. In 1861 Michelet paid him the great compliment of calling him 'l'inventeur de la mer'.

Among his fellow doctors the *Dissertation* was an immediate success. Many of them were convinced by his ideas and began to send their patients to the seaside. Russell's theories were in the tradition of all the popular medical writers, like Wittie and Floyer, who had long been advocating cold bathing and huge drinks of spa water; but he made sea-bathing seem a novel cure by all the portentous solemnity with which he surrounded it. 'A perfect repose of the Body, and calmness of mind, is to be observed before the Use of the Cold Bath', the blood must be prevented from 'flying to the head', the bowels must be 'sound', the pores must be closed – so the colder the weather the better for the bather – and all sorts of other conditions observed before his patients would dare to take a dip. Dr Russell spoke of the sea having a detergent action, and a course of bathing probably did lead to startling improvements in all the invalids whose diseases were due quite simply to dirt.

He continued the analogy with the spas by insisting that not only bathing in the sea, but also drinking sea-water, 'this new medicine', was beneficial, especially early in the morning. Five o'clock was the hour he recommended. Visitors to Bath at that time sometimes drank as many as eighteen glasses of mineral water a day. Dr Russell was slightly less generous in his prescriptions of sea-water. 'A pint', he wrote, 'is commonly sufficient in grown persons, to give three or four sharp stools.' Sometimes the doctor encouraged his patients to go for a trip in a bouncy little boat to complete the treatment. Delicate invalids were allowed to dilute the sea-water with milk, but even taken neat, it cannot, in those days when the sea was infinitely

The Beach at Scarborough
by T. Ramsey, *c.* 1770

less polluted than it is now, have tasted much nastier than some of the sulphurous, stinking spa waters his patients were used to.

The whole *Dissertation* is full of contradictions. Dr Russell describes giving his patients disgusting mediaeval concoctions of crabs' eyes, tar, snails and 'prepared wood-lice', but he was ahead of his time in seeing the virtues of fresh air and exercise for delicate children. 'I have had children sent to me weak, pale, loaded with hair, their necks and throats wrapped up in flannel, and in short the whole texture of the body relaxed by too hot clothing and night sweats; whom I have returned to their parents, bare necked, their heads shaved, the tumours of the neck cured and their whole countenance healthy, after having strengthened them by bathing in the sea.'

In 1753 Dr Russell moved from Lewes to Brighton so that he could personally supervise his patients. He built himself what was then the most imposing house in the town, a big red-brick building conveniently near the beach. People began to flock to Brighton for his cures and other towns near the sea began to realize that rich invalids might bring in more money than fish. The seaside – although the word had not yet been coined – was about to become the rage, and shrewd Dr Russell was rewarded with prestige, wealth and epigrams.

> Admiring ages Russell's
> fame shall know,
> Till Ocean's healing
> waters cease to flow.

Until well after the end of the eighteenth century sea-bathing was generally looked upon as a serious, therapeutic exercise, only to be undertaken, as Gibbon put it, 'after due preparation and advice'. It was something beneficial and rather nasty to be got over before breakfast and the pleasures of the day. Fanny Burney, in spite of having often bathed at Brighton – sometimes, to fulfil the essential condition of having the pores thoroughly closed, in November – did not dare yield to the temptation to take a dip one August day at Sidmouth when the sea was as 'calm and gentle as the Thames'. 'Having no advice at hand, I ran no risk.' It is extraordinary how long some vestiges of Dr Russell's ideas have lasted. There are still people who believe that there is peculiar merit in early morning sea-bathing. They return to breakfast glowing with moral superiority.

The drinking of sea-water was much practised until about the end of the Regency after which it gradually died out, though as late as the 1850s a few doctors were still recommending it mixed with beef-tea or port. At first some

Opposite
Detail from *A morning view of the sands at Worthing* by John Nixon, 1808

17

people drank even more than Russell had suggested. A visitor to Lyme Regis recorded many people coming down to the beach three or four times in as many hours to drink a pint on each occasion.

By the end of the eighteenth century no seaside resort was considered really established until it had its own resident physician. In Jane Austen's unfinished satire *Sanditon* – a book which is extremely illuminating about early seaside resorts – Mr Parker, a passionate seaside enthusiast and promoter, 'was convinced that the advantage of a medical man at hand would materially promote the rise and prosperity of the place – would tend to bring a prodigious influx – nothing else was wanting'.

'Watering-places' was the term used to describe both the spas and the sea-bathing places in the eighteenth and early nineteenth centuries, and in the amusements they provided the new watering-places modelled themselves faithfully on the old. Subscription balls, circulating libraries, rules governing dancing and card playing, even formal gardens, souvenirs and promenades were all borrowed from the spas. The sea-bathing places also adopted some characteristic spa etiquette. Brighton shared for a time a Master of Ceremonies with Bath and Tunbridge Wells, and for a few years bells were rung out, as at Bath, to announce the arrival of newcomers. Mr Wade, the Master of Ceremonies at Brighton, had considerable power in the early years of his reign and could ruin a ball or close a play by withdrawing his patronage. At Blackpool, William Hutton proposed a set of seven rules for the 'infant commonwealth', the first of which was that every visitor should register his name 'as at Buxton'. Even as late as 1820 the Master of Ceremonies at Margate was entreating ladies to enter their names and addresses at the library so that he might call on them. The great debt to the spas is still visible in many old-established English seaside resorts; their Regency crescents and terraces echo those built decades earlier in Bath or Buxton.

Until the spas went into a genteel decline at the beginning of Victoria's reign and the seaside resorts became simultaneously more and more popular, much the same kind of people patronized the old and the new watering-places. But the decorum and formality that were part of Beau Nash's legacy to the spas seem from the start to have been incompatible with the sea air. Cowper in *The Retirement*, which was written in 1782, has a famous description of the new fashion.

Your prudent grandmammas, ye modern belles,
Content with Bristol, Bath and Tunbridge Wells,

When health required it would consent to roam,
Else more attached to pleasures found at home.
But now alike, gay widow, virgin, wife,
Ingenious to diversify dull life,
In coaches, chaises, caravans, and hoys,
Fly to the coast for daily, nightly joys,
And all, impatient of dry land, agree
With one consent to rush into the sea.

The Rush
into the Sea

If bathing itself was not considered a pleasure in the eighteenth century, watching 'fair Naiads plunging in the crystal wave' was one of the delights of the seaside. Innumerable verses were written in praise of Venuses rising from the sea at Hastings, Margate or Scarborough, and it was one of Brighton's boasts that 'the number of beautiful women who every morning court the embraces of the watery God far exceeds that of any watering-place in the kingdom'. The unfamiliar sight of women bathing gave an exhilarating sexiness to the beaches, which was enhanced by the possibility that the ladies might be naked.

Men bathed naked as a matter of course until well into the nineteenth century. The way they stood 'shivering and hesitating, their persons wholly exposed' on the steps of their bathing-machines was considered in the 1840s, 'a stain on the gentility of Brighthelmstone', and it was not until as late as 1871 that local regulations finally forced them into drawers. Women, from the very beginning of the cult of the seaside, could hire long concealing gowns to wear in the water:

> The ladies dressed in flannel cases,
> Show nothing but their handsome faces.

But there seems to have been no strong social pressure making these clammy, enveloping gowns compulsory; and until about the end of the Regency, women sometimes wore nothing at all in the water.

This is not often mentioned in contemporary descriptions of the seaside, but there is enough pictorial evidence to suggest that it must have been fairly common. Caricaturists like Rowlandson, Nixon and Gillray, who drew every fashionable pastime, were attracted by all the bustle and the contrasting types at the seaside. They show fat women being carried ashore from little boats, invalids grimacing as they drink their sea-water, London cits sweating on the beaches with handkerchiefs knotted on their heads, while in the distance there are often little female nudes splashing about in the sea. In Rowlandson's well-known cartoon *Summer Amusements at Margate* some leering men are focusing their spy-glasses on a group of them; and Benjamin West's painting of the bathing-place at Ramsgate, which seems to be a straightforward record rather than satire, also includes women bathing naked.

The occasional glimpse of watery nudity may have been permissible in the late eighteenth century, but it became inconceivable for ladies and gentlemen – and on the whole they were the only people who bathed – to walk naked down the beach. After 1750 a bathing-machine became an absolutely essential part of taking a dip. In some places, Brighton, for instance, they were much the same as the one shown in Setterington's engraving in 1735. The bather climbed fully clothed into a wooden hut on wheels and undressed while a horse pulled the machine into the sea and turned it round so that the door was facing away from the beach. The water was now lapping round the steps and one could descend straight into it.

In 1753 Benjamin Beale, a Margate Quaker, invented a refinement in the interests of decency. This was an awning rather like a giant pram hood which could be lowered until it touched the surface of the water, making a dark,

An engraved trade card advertising Sayer's bathing-machines and bathing-room at Margate, 1791

private patch of sea in which ladies could bathe 'in a manner consistent with the most refined delicacy'. They were soon adopted not only at Margate, but at many other rising sea-bathing places like Lowestoft, Weymouth and Scarborough. Used as they were intended, they must have made bathing very unpleasant; and not surprisingly, women seem often to have cast decency aside and splashed past the claustrophobic awnings into the open sea.

As towards the end of the century, propriety began to seem more important, each sea-bathing place developed its

The Bathing Place at Ramsgate by Benjamin West, *c.* 1780

own rules to keep bathers of different sexes apart. The Master of Ceremonies who controlled bathing at Brighton 'sent the gentlemen 200 yards to the westward' and at Blackpool in 1788 a bell was rung when it was time for the ladies to bathe and the gentlemen to vanish from the sea-front. 'If a gentleman is seen on the parade he forfeits a bottle of wine.' At Southport men had tried approaching the ladies during their bathe by boat, so a system of fines was brought in. If they sailed within thirty yards of the bathers five shillings had to be paid to the poor of the parish. By the beginning of the Regency, the sexes were completely separated in the sea and they were to remain so in England for nearly a hundred years.

Bathing from the machines was expensive. 'The regular price is one shilling each time you bathe, and when you leave off the attendants expect a gratuity nearly equal to the charge of their master, which is generally complied with,' writes the author of the *New Scarborough Guide* at the end of the century. The price seems high – the same guide mentions that full board could be had at the best lodging-house in the town for £1 a week – and it must have had the effect of ensuring that bathing was a pastime only for prosperous visitors, and of keeping undesirable locals off the beaches.

As more people began to visit the seaside and most of them wanted to bathe at the recommended hours between six and nine in the morning, there were often crowds waiting to use the machines. In Brighton unseemly scuffles were reported. People sent their footmen to grab machines as they were drawn out of the sea or even galloped into the water on horseback to claim one. It is not surprising that the number of its bathing-machines became an important status symbol for a sea-bathing place. Scarborough and Margate had by the late 1780s about forty machines each, Ramsgate had twelve, and small seaside towns just beginning to attract a few visitors, like Broadstairs, only one or two.

The owners of fleets of bathing-machines in the popular resorts set up waiting-rooms on the foreshore where, until it was their turn for a machine, bathers could read the papers, gossip and drink their medicinal sea-water, washed down with tea or coffee. These bathing-rooms became almost the equivalent of the pump-rooms at spas – places where the visitors could meet and get to know each other.

It is striking how quickly the whole apparatus of the bathing establishments grew up as soon as visitors began to descend on small coastal towns. Astute local tradesmen realized that there was money to be made from bathing-machines, and fishermen's widows seem to have been particularly quick to grasp the possibilities of the new fashion. At Scarborough the machines were owned by the Widow Field, the Widow Hunter and the Widow Laycock who set up rival establishments at different parts of the bay, and sent noisy touts advertising the virtues of their particular machines and waiting-rooms to meet all the coaches arriving in the town.

The most celebrated people connected with the eighteenth-century bathing establishments were the dippers and bathing-women – the licensed clowns and ogres of the seaside. They took their name from the attendants who had supervised bathing in the mineral springs at the spas, and their role was both to protect their charges from the scaring, unfamiliar sea, and to introduce them to it. They helped the bathers undress in the machines and then, carrying out the instructions of Dr Russell, they would grab them by the shoulders, and in spite of shrieks and pleadings, completely submerge them two or three times in the sea. They chivied the reluctant like hearty old nannies and they seem to have been regarded with a similar affection. 'Smoaker' Miles could get away with pulling the Prince of Wales by the ear when he was swimming out too far at Brighton. He also had a fearsome line in snubs. Once when asked by two dandies where they could get the asses milk which they had been prescribed for their health, he suggested in reply that they should suck each other.

The bathing-women must have been incredibly tough. They stood for hours in flowing skirts and bonnets waist-deep in cold water heaving bathers down the steps of the machines and forcing them for their own good into the sea. They seem, not surprisingly, to have been considered sexless, for though like the male dippers they usually ministered to their own sex, some of their customers were men. In Nixon's cartoon *The Royal Dipping*, the bewildered George III is being splashed by two gleeful and undoubtedly female attendants. John Constable, who called the Brighton bathing-women 'those hideous amphibious animals', said that their 'language both in oaths and voices resembles men'.

Cartoon of Martha Gunn,
c. 1800

Bathing-women like Mrs Glasscock and Mrs Myall of Southend (who advertised her 'particular skill and tenderness'), the Widow Ducker of Scarborough and Mrs Cobby of Brighton became well-known local characters but Martha Gunn became a national legend. She was a landmark of Brighton and, as it says on her gravestone, 'particularly distinguished as a bather in this town for nearly seventy years'. Women of fashion quarrelled over the honour of being dipped by her and she was a particular favourite of the Prince of Wales. When she grew too old and stout to

24

plunge ladies in the sea, she was made beach superintendent, and every morning at six o'clock was at her post on the foreshore. In the last year of her life a visitor said to her, 'Brighton will not look the same without you, Martha.' 'It's like to do without me some day,' she answered; 'but while I have health and life, I am bustling among my old friends and benefactors. I think I ought to be proud, for I've as many bows from man, woman and child as the Prince hisself; aye, I do believe the very dogs of the town know me.'

Her status as a folk heroine is confirmed by her portrayal as a Toby jug, in several different versions, always clutching a flagon of sea-water.

Bathing establishments could be set up quickly, but it took longer for other spa-like amenities to be developed for visitors. Old-established inns were used for dining and cards, but at first dances were sometimes held in the open air, and lodgings were in fishermen's cottages. It was not until twenty-five years after the arrival of Dr Russell that there was any substantial building of new houses in Brighton.

The primitiveness of the decaying fishing ports just beginning a new lease of life as resorts was perhaps part of their charm for the fashionable early visitors to the seaside. There was at this time a growing vogue in England for pastoral simplicity. In their book on Brighton, Osbert Sitwell and Margaret Barton suggested that the new romantic escapism which led aristocratic visitors from London to sleep in sailors' cottages and not mind being tripped up by fishing nets laid out to dry on the Steine was the English equivalent of Marie Antoinette playing at being a shepherdess. Most of the visitors were only too happy when new assembly rooms were built and they could rent comfortable apartments for the season, but if there had been no modish longings for rusticity it is unlikely that so many people would have been prepared to forsake all the comforts of Bath for the novelties of the seaside.

'The best lodgings are most execrable,' wrote the urbane gossip Gilly Williams from Brighton in the 1760s, but, he adds, 'I never liked anything better.' Not everyone, however, relished seaside slumming. The thought of it made Viscount Torrington even more disgruntled than usual. 'That the infirm and the upstart', he wrote in his diaries, 'should resort to these fishing holes, may perhaps be accounted for; but that the healthy owners of parks, good houses and good beds should quit them for the confinements of dirt and misery, appears to me to be downright madness.'

By the 1770s the most popular new resorts like Brighton and Margate had completed the building of essential

Toby jug in the form of Martha Gunn holding a bottle of sea-water, c. 1790

Hall's Library at Margate,
1789

watering-place institutions – assembly rooms, circulating
libraries, theatres and even hot sea-water baths. At Brighton
in 1766 a new assembly room was added to the Castle Inn
and nine years later the landlord of the Old Ship Hotel built
a splendid rival establishment; while at Margate the
elegant assembly rooms had a subscription list of 930 in
1769, the year it opened. Hot salt-water baths to make the
cure less spartan, Mitchener's at Margate and Dr Awsiter's
at Brighton, were built in the 1760s. At Brighton travelling
companies of actors had performed in barns in the sixties
and a pretty, permanent theatre was opened in 1774; the new
Theatre Royal at Margate was one of the finest in the
provinces, 'built after the model of Covent Garden'.

In every town trying to turn itself into a sea-bathing place
one particular walk, like the broad, grassy Steine at Brighton,
was adopted for fashionable promenading. Here in the
evening everyone strolled about bowing to their new

26

aquaintances. It was the place where one went 'to be stared at and stare'.

The new circulating libraries, by now grandly known as marine circulating libraries, were perhaps most important to the social life of a new resort. They did not just lend out books, but also sold novelties, organized raffling – which had long been a popular pastime at the spas – and soon built rooms for cards, billiards and concerts. When visitors first arrived, they paid a subscription which allowed them to use all the library's facilities, and writing their name in the library visitors' book was a way of introducing themselves to the town. It was simply assumed, as it was at the spas, that anyone with the leisure and funds to uproot themselves and stay at the seaside would be socially acceptable to the other visitors. 'Prosperity to the gentry who visit Eastbourne', is the motto engraved on the metal token they got in exchange for their money at Fisher's Library at Eastbourne.

At Margate, Hall's Library had a sophisticated Adam-inspired interior with Corinthian columns and classical busts, and at Brighton there was a flourishing marine library as early as 1760, built by a Mr Baker of Tunbridge Wells. Ladies used to sit on the verandah reading and listening to a booming band of trombones and French horns, which does not seem to have stopped them overhearing interesting titbits of scandal.

> For whilst you discourse,
> to each word that is said,
> Attentive they listen, and
> *seem* but to read.

By the 1770s two new libraries had been opened in competition with Baker's and round them grew up little shops stocked with expensive trifles, lace, china and ribbons. The shopkeepers soon learned to put up their prices to suit the prosperity of their visitors; it was also often subtly suggested that the trinkets were smuggled, which made them seem great bargains.

The earliest seaside visitors, like all their successors, seem to have felt the urge to buy keepsakes that would remind them of the pleasures of their stay long after they had returned home. This habit had begun at the spas. Bath never developed a specialized souvenir trade, but Tunbridge Wells was already by the end of the seventeenth century famous for what Celia Fiennes called its 'delicate, neate and thin ware of wood'. Candlesticks, cribbage boards, inkstands, pin-cushions and so on made of turned

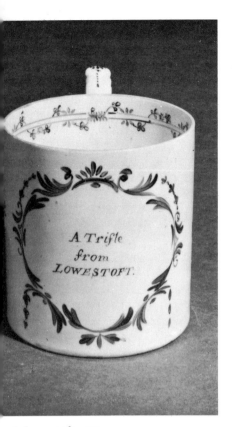

A Lowestoft mug
painted in enamel colours,
c. 1795

and painted or inlaid wood were sold to visitors to the Wells. It was 'the custom to take Tunbridge fairings to their friends at home'; and as soon as people started to visit the South coast, seaside shops there began to stock Tunbridge ware. Towards the end of the century it was being decorated with suitable mottoes; 'A Present from Margate' or 'A Brighton Trifle', and by the end of the Regency more Tunbridge ware was being sold in Brighton than in Tunbridge itself. It was quite expensive (a workbox cost £1 4s. in 1766) but this did not deter the prosperous people who could afford to frequent watering-places.

The most elegant seaside souvenirs of the eighteenth century were the mugs and jugs made at the porcelain works at Lowestoft. In the 1780s, when Lowestoft was a growing resort, they began to be painted with the motto 'A Trifle from Lowestoft'. But the firm also produced almost as many 'trifles' from insignificant nearby inland towns like Bungay and Holt, so the market for souvenirs at a minor sea-bathing place like Lowestoft cannot yet have been much larger than that in any small town. But also by the 1780s the little oval enamel patch-boxes produced at Bilston in Staffordshire were being decorated with mottoes especially for the seaside market. Their lids often had transfer prints of views of places like Weymouth or Scarborough applied to them, or were painted with flowers and the words 'A Present from . . .'. And by the Regency quantities of souvenir mugs decorated with views of the Steine or Weymouth sands were being produced in Staffordshire to be sold at the seaside, and buying souvenirs had become part of the pattern of a visit to the coast.

There were two main reasons why some resorts grew quickly while others only attracted comparatively few visitors from nearby counties; the first was accessibility from London, or other large cities, and the second was royal patronage, for the presence of even the most disreputable royal duke always seems to have meant at the very least a temporary increase in the number of fashionable visitors.

In those days of bad roads and uncomfortable, expensive coaches, the length of the journey to a watering-place was an important consideration. Mr Parker in *Sanditon* boasts that his pet resort is, 'The most desirable distance from London. One complete, measured mile nearer than East Bourne. Only conceive, Sir, the advantage of saving a whole Mile, in a long Journey.' Except for Scarborough, which had a long-established clientele of northern gentry, the most popular eighteenth-century resorts tended to be those in Kent and Sussex, the coastal areas nearest to London.

A Bilston enamel
patch-box, c 1790

28

Margate in Kent was in a unique position for it could easily be reached by boat from London, and as soon as the rush into the sea began, the Margate hoys, cargo boats which had for many years been sailing up the Thames to London packed with fish to return with provisions, started to take passengers wishing to sample the seaside. The hoys were notoriously uncomfortable and the journey could take two or three days in bad weather, but at half-a-crown a trip they were far cheaper than the more reliable coaches and they did 'incredible business'.

Margate was a huge success with the London cits. They 'haughtily strutted about, bending their heads backwards for the dread of being thought to have contracted a sneaking stoop behind the counter'. Though Margate's new buildings were outstandingly elegant and many fashionable people visited the town in the eighteenth century, gradually its very success made them discriminate against it. One never knew who one might meet at the marine library.

All sorts of upstarts had always gone to the spas to try their luck, but Margate, because of the hoys, became the first resort where it seemed to contemporaries that tradesmen, shopkeepers and other members of the middle classes out-numbered the gentry. The crowds of 'cits' and 'dowdies' who went there at the end of the eighteenth century were the sort of people who would never have stayed even for a few days at Tunbridge Wells or Bath, though they might well have spent jolly Sundays dancing and drinking tea at the London spas like Bagnigge Wells. John Gilpin in Cowper's poem who had never thought of taking a single weekday's holiday in 'twice-ten tedious years' was just the kind of person who by the 1790s was being persuaded by his wife that perhaps they could afford to take a few days off to sample the gaieties of Margate.

Margate continued to grow almost as rapidly as Brighton, but by the beginning of the nineteenth century it was being described as 'a well frequented, if not fashionable, watering-place'. 'Lord, Madam,' says a snob in an 1820s cartoon, 'you can never think of going to Margate – it is so common.' Gay, crowded Margate had become an early example of those fluctuating social distinctions between seaside resorts which are such a characteristic and ludicrous part of their history.

Weymouth was a small, quiet coastal town whose popularity was immensely increased by royal patronage; but when this ceased it faded again into insignificance because of its distance from London. Its fame began when George III, who was recovering from his first attack of madness, was advised by his doctors that Weymouth was a suitable place to take the sea-water cure.

In 1789 the royal party arrived to be greeted with huge jubilation. Fanny Burney describes it: 'The loyalty of this place is excessive; they have dressed out every street with labels of "God Save the King": all the shops have it over their doors; all the children wear it in their caps; all the labourers in their hats; and all the sailors *in their voices* . . .' When it was finally decided that the king was ready to take a plunge in the sea, the bathing-women had 'God Save the King' in the bandeaux of their bonnets and in large letters round their waists. 'When first I surveyed these loyal nymphs it was with some difficulty that I kept my features in order,' wrote Miss Burney. 'Nor', she went on, 'was this all. Think but of the surprise of His Majesty, the first time of his bathing; he had no sooner popped his royal head under the water than a band of music concealed in a neighbouring machine struck up God save Great George our King.' This comic scene is depicted in Nixon's print *The Royal Dipping*.

Poor George was delighted by Weymouth. 'I have never enjoyed a sight so pleasing,' he said as he walked along the sands. He was also very touched by all the demonstrations

George III's first bathe at Weymouth in 1789 – the scene described by Fanny Burney. Cartoon by John Nixon

30

of loyalty, and for as long as he was well enough he made annual visits to the town. His wife and family did not share his taste. 'This place is more dull and stupid than I can find words to express,' wrote Princess Mary, from Weymouth in 1798, 'Sophia and me do not intend to honour the sea with *our charmes* this year.' However, many of his loyal and respectable subjects happily followed his example.

The royal party were not directly very profitable to local tradesmen, for the king always insisted on bringing all his provisions with him.

> Bread, cheese, salt, catchup, vinegar and mustard,
> Small beer and bacon, apple pie and custard,
> All, all from Windsor greets his frugal Grace,
> For Weymouth is a d – mned expensive place.

Other seaside towns benefited from the visits of members of the royal family, for instance Worthing expanded after Princess Amelia, the youngest daughter of George III, went there in 1798 and the visits of Queen Caroline and her daughter to Southend made the town quite fashionable and were followed by much building. Sidmouth, in Devon, which was a small out-of-the-way village when George III stayed there for a short time in 1781, became an elegant resort, a favourite of Queen Victoria's parents. This whole phenomenon was to be repeated again and again on the Continent in the nineteenth century, and cunning efforts were constantly being made to tempt royal visitors. As William Hutton remarked; 'Majesty moving over the face of the waters inspires them with fresh influence.'

Of course, the most striking example of the happy effects of royal patronage is Brighton. The presence of the Prince of Wales combined with the fact that Brighton was only fifty miles from London and had already had a great boost from Dr Russell to give it a dazzling advantage over all other seaside resorts. It eclipsed Bath to become the most fashionable place in England, the glittering 'Queen of Watering-places' – and the inspiration of innumerable historical romances.

Brighton

In 1783 when he was twenty-one George, Prince of Wales, came to Brighton for the first time at the invitation of his uncle the Duke of Cumberland. The town greeted him, not with bands concealed in bathing-machines, but with gun salutes, fireworks, stag-hunts and the most brilliant ball that had ever been held there. His visit was short, but he told everyone how delighted he had been with the place and returned the following year surrounded by friends as stylish and reckless as himself. Brighton seemed the perfect setting for their escapades. They gambled, pursued actresses, ran up huge debts, sang ballads, got drunk and played fatuous practical jokes. The *Morning Post* commented the following summer: 'The visit of a certain gay, illustrious character at Brighton has frightened away a number of old maids who used constantly to frequent that place. The history of the gallantries of the last season, which is constantly in circulation, has something in it so voluminous and tremendous to boot, that the old tabbies shake in their shoes whenever his R – H – is mentioned.'

A few 'old tabbies' may have packed up and gone to Weymouth or Worthing, but there was an immense increase in the number of smarter and less respectable visitors to the town. At first all the glamorous people seemed to melt away when the Prince went back to London. In 1784 *The Brighthelmstone Intelligence* complained that the town had 'within the last few days become a desert; scarce a person of fashion remaining'. But as he continued to spend his summers there, the number of fashionable visitors shot up. In 1787 it was reported that there were twice as many visitors as in the preceding year, and by 1794 the town was so crowded that people slept in post-chaises and bathing-machines.

The Prince's liking for Brighton became a more or less

Beauties of BRIGHTON

permanent attachment when he fell in love with Mrs Fitzherbert. He had met her there, and after their secret marriage in 1785 Brighton seemed the best place for them to set up house. Their life together began with an idyllic summer of 'abject poverty' in a rented farmhouse; and although the Prince was incapable of keeping his resolution to live in rustic simplicity, he remained faithful to Brighton. For the next eight years he came down there regularly, and this was perhaps the gayest period in the town's history.

Many ingredients combined. to make up the special flavour of late-eighteenth-century Brighton. One of them was a passionate horsiness. The bare, rolling Downs that surrounded the town were perfect for the most dashing displays of riding and driving, and the streets of the town became the best place in England to show off a new carriage. Hunting had long been a favourite pastime there – even Dr Johnson had indulged in it while he was staying with the Thrales and had been complimented on the 'good firmness' of his seat – but the Prince and his set were

High society promenading on the Steine in 1826. Including the Duke of York and the Duke of Gloucester, Nathanial Rothschild the banker and, far left, Talleyrand who was then ambassador to London. By A. Crowquill, Esq., etched by Cruikshank

33

crazy about driving. They spent much of their time racing dangerously through the town and over the Downs in their phaetons and curricles. Some of his friends were totally obsessed with the art; Sir John Lade, for instance, ended his life socially ruined but perfectly happy as a public coachman on the London to Brighton run.

George himself, before he became so fat that he had to be hoisted on to the saddle by a special machine, was famous for his horsemanship. In 1784 he made a record-breaking ride from London to Brighton and back in only ten hours, and it was typical of him that the first of the fantastic, oriental buildings he commissioned at Brighton was the royal stables. It cost £54,000 and with its great glass dome and Indian decoration was, as he often said, a palace for horses. The clothes of the smart young men who followed him to the seaside reflected their preoccupations. 'It is somewhat difficult to determine which the fashionable tribe most resemble,' complained the *Morning Post*, 'a set of *grooms* or a company of *smugglers*.'

The Brighton races became a social highlight of the summer, and in the first years of the nineteenth century a new kind of riding suddenly became the thing with visiting ladies who 'enjoyed anything singular'. On sunny mornings the cliffs were crowded with donkeys weighed down with modish women of all shapes and sizes clutching parasols. The fashion did not last long, but the donkeys remained to become one of the traditions of the English seaside.

Brighton society was also enlivened by a growing number of aristocratic visitors from France. Although the town had no real harbour, so that all the passengers and their luggage had to be rowed from the packets to the shore, the Dieppe to Brighton route was then one of the best ways of getting from Paris to London. As early as 1764 Gilly Williams was commenting on the number of French people staying in Brighton 'extraordinary exotics . . . barbers, milliners, barons, counts arrive here almost every tide'. Later the Prince invited many French nobles, like the Duc d'Orleans and the Princesse de Lamballe, to stay with him at the Pavilion. They entered horses for the races and relished the carefree sophistication of the town. For the first and last time in their history, an English seaside resort was considered smart by the chicest members of continental high society.

By 1789 the first fugitives from the Revolution were beginning to arrive, and in the next few years Brighton constantly buzzed with stories of marquises appearing disguised as sailors and comtesses concealed in coils of rope. Four years later war was declared between France and

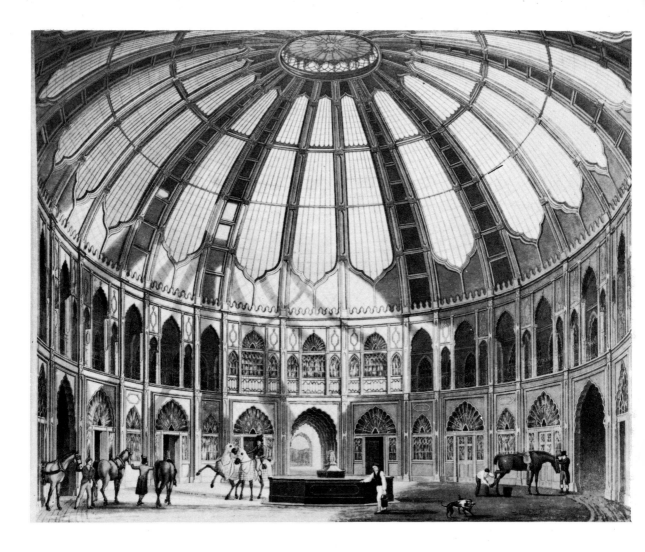

England, and from then until after Waterloo (except for a rush of visitors to France in 1802, many of whom were arrested when war broke out again) travel abroad for pleasure virtually ceased. The English watering-places, particularly Brighton, gained the custom of many of the wealthy people who might otherwise have been going to Paris or on the Grand Tour, for even when the country was at war life in the pleasure resorts went on much as before.

At Brighton the gaieties were intensified by the presence of soldiers camped on the Downs. Their continual parades, sham fights and manoeuvres were looked upon as entertainments rather than preparations for invasion. Military bands cheered the town with their stirring tunes – beginning another seaside tradition – and the Prince's own regiment attracted all the most dandified young officers in the

Interior of the Royal
Stables from John Nash's
Brighton Pavilion, 1820–25

35

country. Brighton became the dream of every silly, flirtatious girl, like Jane Austen's Lydia in *Pride and Prejudice*. 'In Lydia's imagination, a visit to Brighton comprized every possibility of earthly happiness. She saw with the creative eye of fancy, the streets of that gay bathing-place covered with officers. She saw herself the object of attention, to tens and to scores of them at present unknown. She saw all the glories of the camp; its tents stretched forth in beauteous uniformity of lines, crowded with the young and the gay, and dazzling with scarlet; and to complete the view, she saw herself seated beneath a tent, tenderly flirting with at least six officers at once.'

Jane Austen herself disapproved of Brighton and the whole fast and superficial style of living which the town had come to epitomize. 'I assure you', she wrote in a letter of 1799, 'that I dread the idea of going to Brighton as much as you do, but I am not without hope that something may happen to prevent it.' She was not alone in disliking the idleness and dissipation of the place. The Rev John Styles taking 'the sea is His and He made it' as his text, gave a famous sermon on the perils of the seaside in general and Brighton in particular. 'Many young persons,' he thundered, 'now lost to society, have to attribute their ruin to a career of novel reading begun at a watering-place.'

But crowds continued to arrive, attracted rather than repelled by its reputation, and prices rose steeply so that before the beginning of the Regency there were already complaints that Brighton was far more expensive than London. In 1785 a single room could be had for a guinea a week and a house on the Steine for eight or ten guineas, the charges in 1796 ranged from 2s. 6d. a night for a stable to £20 a week for a house.

The Prince himself led the spending. He ran up huge bills with local tradesmen, bankrupting some of them in the process, contributed lavishly to local charities and made a habit of entertaining the whole town on his birthdays with fireworks, roast oxen and hogsheads of beer. It was, however, in the continual alterations to his house, culminating in the exotic splendour of Nash's final design, that his wild extravagance was most conspicuous.

The early versions of the Pavilion had a direct influence on other seaside buildings. In 1789 the Prince has his modest farmhouse rebuilt by Henry Holland. The Marine Pavilion, as it was now called, was a charming house in the Palladian manner with a central domed rotunda and wings with long bow-windows overlooking the Steine. Clifford Musgrave in his book *Life in Brighton* writes: 'The creation of the Marine Pavilion gave an enormous fillip to house-building in Brighton, and in the years that followed

Opposite
The roofs of John Nash's Royal Pavilion

37

Rex Whistler's modern allegory *H.R.H. The Prince Regent Awakening the Spirit of Brighton*, 1944

the completion of the Prince's residence the combined features of curved bays, long windows and iron railings became charmingly characteristic not only of hundreds of houses that were built during the next few years in the town, but in those of many other seaside resorts such as Hastings, Ramsgate, Margate, Weymouth, and eventually in towns all over the British Isles.' Between 1801 and 1804 the Pavilion was extended again, and Holland's pupil Robinson added to its bow-windows the shell-like canopies which were to become another distinctive feature of Regency architecture at the seaside.

In all its transformations the Pavilion reflected the exquisite taste and originality which were facets of George's complex personality. He played as important a part in its changing character as the architects and decorators he employed, supervising every stage of the designs and insisting on alterations and rearrangements until just the effect he wanted had been achieved.

He continually redecorated the interior of the Pavilion, and after 1802, inspired by a gift of Chinese wallpaper, the rooms became more and more oriental in character. But this did not satisfy him and in about 1805 he made the decision to change his house completely. He no longer wanted a simple seaside villa, but a sumptuous, oriental palace.

He rejected the first two designs he commissioned, one of them, by William Porden, Chinese-inspired, and the other by Humphrey Repton in the newly fashionable Indian manner. This was partly on account of his usual financial difficulties, but perhaps more because they were too dry for his taste and lacked the individuality and charm he was looking for. He finally chose Nash's design in 1815. It transformed the shell of the original classical Pavilion

38

into a dream palace with onion domes, minarets, fretwork tracery and parapets – neither Chinese nor Indian, but a quite original Arabian Nights fantasy.

George as Regent at last had an income large enough to indulge his love of building, but he had become bloated and unpopular. Brighton itself no longer seemed to raise his spirits and he had finally discarded Mrs Fitzherbert, replacing her by a succession of fat grandmothers. It was now the excitement of creating the new Royal Pavilion that made him keep coming back to the town. The Pavilion became an escape, a private world of splendour and romance where he could cut himself off from the mockery of his subjects.

The interior is unlike any other. Huge lotus-like lamps hang from writhing dragons, ceilings are painted like delicate morning skies or gleam with fish scales, palm trees seem to shoot through the kitchen floors or arch their leaves over the banqueting room, there is bamboo everywhere and chairs shaped like dolphins. It is all so magnificently self-confident and theatrical that it transcends vulgarity.

Nash managed his magical effects by using all the latest technical developments and newest materials. The feeling of lightness which prevents the richness of the decoration from being overpowering could only have been achieved by the use of cast iron. It provides frames for the onion domes, and, masquerading as palm trees or bamboo, is used for the slender columns that support the building.

The Pavilion, brilliantly lit by gas – another innovation – and kept as hot as a Turkish bath by patent stoves, was the setting for enormous banquets and private concerts. 'I do not believe', wrote the bitchy Princesse de Lieven, 'that since the days of Heliogabalus there has been such magnificence and luxury. There is something effeminate in it which is disgusting. One spends the evening half-lying on cushions; the lights are dazzling; there are perfumes, music, liqueurs.'

Three years before his death, when every detail of the Pavilion had been completed, George IV (as he was by then) became completely bored with Brighton, suddenly jaded by the crowds, the houses which now clustered round his palace, and the whole rakish flavour of the place which he had done so much to create. He never visited it again but by now the town could do very well without him. Brighton had become 'London-super-mare'. Its population was increasing more rapidly than that of any other town in the country, speculators were rushing up terraces and crescents, and every day over forty fast public coaches brought down yet more people from London.

Nash's Royal Pavilion has a special place in the history of the seaside. Though it was in one sense a unique building without either past or future, it was the first and best of those

The new fashion for donkey
riding, 1805

completely personal follies which, in Europe and America as well as in England, were to be built by the sea. It was constantly ridiculed by the Regent's contemporaries. 'One would think St. Paul's Cathedral had come down to Brighton and pupped,' is Sidney Smith's famous quip. 'The Kremlin', wrote Cobbett, using one of its politer nicknames, 'has long been the subject of laughter all over the country.' In Victoria's reign it was gutted and used for flower shows, council meetings and exhibitions of 'natural deformities'. It only began to be appreciated and restored in the 1920s. But in spite of this, its exotic silhouette of domes and minarets was imprinted on the English imagination as the perfect setting for seaside pleasures. It had an unacknowledged but pervasive influence on the subsequent look of resorts. In the Edwardian Golden Age of the English seaside, bands played under onion domes, filigree cast iron edged the promenade, and scores of crude, miniature Royal Pavilions were built for concert parties and fortune-tellers at the end of piers.

The Romantic Seaside

Of all the changes that had been going on at the English seaside between the 1730s and the beginning of the Victorian age, perhaps the most striking was a change in people's attitude to the sea itself, in what they expected to feel when they looked at it. The earliest visitors to Scarborough and Brighton would have seen little reason to look at it at all. They did not sit for hours staring at the waves – to linger on the beach was considered a pointless occupation, 'to the detriment of his shoes and the diminution of his patience'. To them, as to previous generations, the sea was far too frightening and formless to be beautiful – a pleasant enough sight on a fine day, perhaps, but nothing more (and if they were seriously taking the sea-water cure, it must have been difficult not to regard it as a distasteful expanse of nasty medicine).

It was not until the middle of the eighteenth century that poets and men of letters began to appreciate and reveal to their readers the grandeur and power of untamed nature – mountains especially, but also the sea. Edmund Burke in the 1750s had defined 'the sublime', which rather than 'the beautiful' was 'productive of the strongest emotions the mind is capable of'. Grand, vast and terrifying, the sea was a perfect example of the sublime; and it began, in its variety, its strength, the contrast between its benevolent calms and appalling storms to seem a fitting image for the power of God or of Nature. Cowper in *The Retirement* followed his witty, satirical description of 'the rush into the sea' with the lines:

> Oceans exhibit fathomless and broad,
> Much of the power and majesty of God . . .
> Vast as it is, it answers as it flows
> The breathings of the lightest air that blows,

Curling and whit'ning over all the waste,
The rising waves obey the increasing blast,
Abrupt and horrid as the tempest roars,
Thunder and flash upon the steadfast shores
'Till he that rides the whirlwind checks the rein
Then all the world of waters sleeps again—

By the early nineteenth century, the sea had become one of the favourite themes of the Romantic poets. For both Byron and Shelley it had an endless fascination. To them it spoke not only of perpetually changing life but also of annihilation. In 1818 Shelley wrote a poem full of despairing longing for a quiet death which ends with the lines:

– and hear the sea
Breathe o're my dying brain its last monotony.

He was drowned four years later when his boat the *Don Juan* was wrecked in a storm off the Italian coast; and his death itself, which he had foreseen and perhaps courted, seems a fitting symbol of the high Romantic attitude to the sea – the poet was united at last with the most mysterious of all the forces of Nature.

Artists, who since the seventeenth century had generally ignored the sea, returned to the subject with a new enthusiasm, and by the 1820s there were complaints that the walls of the Academy were so full of seascapes, shipwrecks and fishing-boats at anchor that there was little room for landscapes. Turner was obsessed with the sea and many of his greatest pictures are seascapes. He painted it with marvellous intensity in all its moods and even in his most abstract studies of light and spray there is a sense of this new Romantic feeling for its sublime mystery and grandeur.

The aesthetic discovery of the sea very soon became a fashion. The language of Burke and the Romantics became a cliché of the guide-books and a convention of polite conversation. 'A singular, but yet awful combination of the pleasing and the sublime', is the description of a stormy day in a Regency guide to Blackpool. In *Sanditon*, Sir Edward Denham, a silly, literary young man, repeats all the right sentiments. 'He began in a tone of great taste and feeling to talk of the Sea and the Seashore – and ran with great energy through all the usual phrases employed in praise of their sublimity and descriptive of the *undescribable* emotions they excite in the Mind of Sensibility.'

The promise of these 'undescribable emotions' seems to have become almost as important as fashion and health in making people want to visit the seaside, and once they got

44

Vessel in Distress off Yarmouth, Turner, 1831

there nobody was surprised if young ladies wept at their first sight of the ocean – in fact, it was almost expected of them. When Charlotte Brontë went to Bridlington for the first time, 'she could not speak till she had shed some tears'.

This new Romantic attitude was not generally reflected in resort architecture until the first years of the nineteenth century, but it then began to have an immense effect on the whole look of the English coast. Fishing villages and ports had traditionally been built with their houses huddled together for protection, turning their backs on the sea. Hastings, for instance, was a typical old seaside town. Its narrow High Street ran inland in a valley between cliffs. In the last decade of the eighteenth century some of the small, ancient fishermen's houses were replaced by more elegant ones for visitors, but it was not until the Regency that

45

crescents and squares were built parallel with the coastline and houses with fine views of the sea began to appear on the cliff tops.

In Brighton many of the late-eighteenth-century developments, like Russell Square, faced inland, but in 1808 Royal Crescent, the first group of houses overlooking the sea, was completed, and in the next thirty years the town spread out along the coast in mile after mile of fine new terraces and crescents. All the grandest and most desirable of these new houses had big windows overlooking the water, and by the beginning of the Victorian age a sea view had already become a priceless asset to any lodging-house or rented apartment. Draughts might howl through the rooms and the windows might rattle endlessly, the sun reflected off the sea might dazzle in the drawing-room – but no matter – now the visitors could contemplate the waves as they ate their breakfast and relish at a safe distance 'all the grandeur of the storm'.

The wish to build houses close to the sea happily coincided with the discovery, at the end of the eighteenth century, of an inexpensive and effective way of protecting their brickwork. Stone was by then too expensive and scarce a material to be used by seaside speculative builders, but now brick houses could be faced with stucco, which had recently been perfected, and would no longer be ruined by the damp and the salt spray. Some of the earliest houses overlooking the sea, like those in Royal Crescent, had been protected with shiny black tiles that gleam like mussel shells in the sunlight, but by the Regency most of the large new seaside developments were faced with stucco. It gives a characteristic brilliance and unity to the buildings of Brighton and many lesser early-nineteenth-century resorts.

Parades began to be built along the edge of the sea so that as people strolled about in the conventional watering-place manner they could look at the ocean as well as nod and bow to their new acquaintances, and before Victoria came to the throne most fashionable seaside resorts had at least the beginnings of a promenade lined with bright new houses overlooking the water.

The more people went to the seaside to be inspired by untamed Nature, the more urban and tamer the coast became. Some true Romantics disliked the paradoxical mixture. 'What are they doing here?' wrote Charles Lamb of stockbrokers at the seaside, 'if they had true relish of the ocean, why have they brought all this land luggage with them? . . . What mean these scanty book-rooms – marine libraries as they entitle them – if the sea were, as they would have us believe, "a book to read strange matter in"? What are their foolish concert-rooms, if they come, as they would

fain be thought to do, to listen to the music of the waves? All is false and hollow pretention.'

John Constable, who painted some beautiful oil sketches of Brighton, also felt that, 'the magnificence of the sea . . . its everlasting voice, is drowned in the din and lost in the tumult of stagecoaches – gigs – "flys" etc.' But this new feeling of wonder at the sight of the sea was not lost, even in all the bustle and noise of nineteenth-century resorts. In the nineteenth century thousands of the people who came to the coast were having their first sight of the ocean, they had not grown up with it as a familiar part of their childhood. Their sense of wonder may have been in part a second-hand, fashionable response, but to many Victorians it was a real emotion and a background to all their seaside pleasures.

There was another idea that played a large part in bringing people to the seaside. This was medical rather than aesthetic – English doctors began to claim that the sea air and the climate of the coast were even more beneficial to invalids than sea-bathing and sea-water drinking. The theory had been formulated in the eighteenth century and gained ground enormously as the nineteenth century progressed.

Lewes Crescent, Brighton, c. 1838, showing the grand stucco houses overlooking the sea and the Chain Pier in the background. Watercolour by G. B. Campion

47

Right at the start of the fashion for the seaside, Dr Relhan, the man who had taken over the famous Dr Russell's thriving practice, had publicized the merits of Brighton's air and climate. Brighton, he wrote, was so free from the 'insalutory vapour of stagnant water' and the 'noxious steam of perspiring trees' that its climate could only be compared with that of Elysium. The merits of pure sea breezes were stressed by other eighteenth-century doctors, but it was not until the 1820s and 1830s, when a spate of immensely detailed and wearisome works of medical topography began to be published, that these theories made much difference to life at the English seaside. Books with titles like *The Sanative Influence of Climate: with an account of the best places of resort for invalids in England, the South of Europe etc.* were astonishingly popular. They were full of tables showing comparative temperatures and humidity, reports of the habits of prevailing winds and discussions of subtle climatic changes from one part of a town to another — even from street to street. A house on top of the cliffs would suit one type of invalid, while those suffering from a different disease would be required to lodge as near the sea as possible to receive the full benefits of the 'dry, elastic' air.

Even the sensible Dr Granville was emphatic on the subject: 'I attach great importance and always have paid great attention to the topographical climate of a sea-bathing place; and even to the particular exposition of the dwelling houses for invalids.' (Dr Granville's book *The Spas of England and Principal Sea-Bathing Places*, which was first published in 1841, is anything but wearisome, it is a fascinating description of his tour round the English resorts and is full of interesting incidental descriptions of life at the seaside at the very beginning of the Victorian age.)

Taking the sea air became one of the main excuses for visiting the seaside, and this meant that after the Regency, although the early spartan habit of bathing in the coldest possible weather had been generally discarded, people again began to come to the seaside in the autumn and winter. Fashionable nineteenth-century English resorts did not close down at the end of the summer season. Most of the pleasure-seekers may have gone, but the invalids remained; and as the thick, suffocating fogs of the Industrial Revolution began to descend on London, escaping for a few weeks of the autumn and winter to the sparkling atmosphere of the seaside seemed more and more desirable, even to people in the best of health.

To the victims of consumption, that scourge of the nineteenth century, a change of air often seemed to offer a

Opposite
A Back-Side and Front View of a Modern Fine Lady or Swimming Venus at Ramsgate, 1805

A Fashionable Dip

Side way or any Way

A BACK-SIDE and FRONT View of a Modern FINE

The Fair Invalid from
*Brighton : The Road, The
Place, The People*, 1862

last hope; and many of them came to the seaside, only to die there in lonely furnished rooms. Ann Brontë arrived in Scarborough a few days before her death. She half-believed that the air there might revive her and longed to have a last look at a place where she had been happy. She had the strength to go for a gentle drive along the sands in a donkey-cart and spent her last evening in a chair by the window gazing at a magnificent sunset. 'Her face was illuminated almost as much as the glorious scenes she gazed upon. Little was said, for it was plain that her thoughts were driven by the imposing view before her to penetrate forwards to the regions of unfading glory.' When she died, the landlady was so practised at seeing that the pleasures of her other guests were not disturbed by a death upstairs, that, 'dinner was announced as ready, through the half-opened door as the living sister was closing the eyes of the dead one'.

Seaside churchyards are full of the graves of sad young girls who had gone into a decline and died far from home.

> Blessed with soft airs and health-restoring skys,
> Sidmouth, to thee the drooping patient flys,

is the inscription on a memorial in a Sidmouth church.

The mildness of the West Country made it seem particularly beneficial to consumptives, and Dr Granville draws a depressing picture of Torquay where the quiet was shattered only by the 'frequent tolling of the funeral bell'. Here is his description of a night in a hotel there: 'The sight of a "spitting pot" as a regular article of furniture, by the side of those which generally adorn a washing-stand, speaks volumes to my imagination. . . . At dawn the sound of a cavernous cough, short, large, and followed by quick and ready expectoration, resounded from the bed-chamber on my left. . . . It seemed to be the cough of a female. On the right, the adjoining bedroom had been the place whence a long sibulating cough – dry, exasperating and nervous, had been heard every five minutes through the short night I had allowed myself, namely from two to six o'clock. . . . Some dozen asses passed before my window, even at that early hour, driven from one great house to another for the purpose, no doubt, of administering their healing milk to invalids.'

Dr Granville was dissatisfied with Torquay. He wanted to discover the ideal seaside location for tubercular patients, a place that would be 'a real Montpellier on the South coast of England'. He thought he had found it in Bournemouth, which a local landowner was just beginning to develop into a resort. Dr Granville offered all sorts of advice on its planning and energetically publicized its virtues. 'I look upon

Bournemouth and its yet unformed colony as a perfect discovery among the sea-nooks one longs to have for a real invalid.' He succeeded almost too well, for as the local paper complained, there was soon a danger that invalids would quite outnumber all other visitors and the place would become, 'a very Metropolis of Bath Chairs'.

'Interesting invalids' and pale, delicate children being wheeled slowly along the promenade were a familiar sight, not only at places like Torquay, Bournemouth and Sidmouth, but at every seaside resort. Hospitals for chest diseases, like the enormous one at Ventnor, were built overlooking the sea, and innumerable schools, which advertised the healthy sea air as an important part of the curriculum, were set up in seaside towns – in Brighton in 1851 there were at least 200 private schools.

Dickens in *Dombey and Son* has little Paul sent down to Brighton for his health. Pushed by 'an old, crab-faced man, in a suit of battered oilskin', and with his sister walking by his side 'he went down to the margin of the ocean every day, and there he would sit or lie in his carriage for hours together: never so distressed as by the company of children – Florence alone excepted, always.' Dickens, like the Romantic poets before him, uses the sea here as an image of death and of eternal life. 'Very often, in the midst of their talk, he would break off, to try to understand what it was that the waves were always saying; and would rise up in his couch to look towards that invisible region far away.'

It comforted the early Victorians to think that, if the pure air could not help their sick children, at least they were spending their last days gazing at the sea; and that perhaps the waves spoke to them as they did to Paul Dombey with vague promises of immortality.

Some people, even before the end of the eighteenth century, wanted all the benefits of the seaside without the bustle and noise, not so much because they were looking for a peaceful setting in which to contemplate untamed Nature or recover their health in the pure sea air, as in order to escape the flashy crowds and moral dangers of Brighton and Margate; and very soon a few resorts began to meet their demand and specialize in seclusion and refinement.

In 1784 Sir Richard Hotham, an energetic businessman who had made a fortune out of selling hats, decided to spend it on founding a select sea-bathing place. He christened it Hothampton, after himself, but the name did not stick and it became known as Bognor. A group of fine houses was built – he called the grandest of them 'The Dome', hoping perhaps to attract a prince. By the time he died in 1799 he had spent over £60,000 on his new town. It did not turn out to be quite as profitable or aristocratic as he had hoped, but it was certainly quiet. 'It is a place calculated for the highest ranks of society, who possessing their separate establishments associate little with each other; and seem to retire here from the bustle of the world, on purpose to enjoy quiet and the pure breezes of the watery element.'

Resorts like Worthing, Broadstairs and Cromer also made a point of not providing any facilities which might attract the rowdy and rakish, and they had a steady flow of timid, respectable visitors. 'There are no places of public amusement, no rooms, balls, nor card assemblies. A small circulating library, consisting chiefly of a few novels, is all that can be offered; but still for such as make retirement their aim, it is certainly an eligible situation.' That is a description of Cromer at the beginning of the nineteenth century. How sadly disappointing it must have been for marriageable daughters to discover that their longed-for visit to the seaside was to be spent at Worthing or Cromer, not Brighton or Scarborough.

In parts of the country where there were no conveniently placed fishing villages waiting to be rejuvenated with bathing-machines and stucco terraces, completely new towns, purpose-built for visitors, were founded on what had once been empty stretches of coast. Bognor and Bournemouth were examples of this sort of seaside speculation, and so were Southport, New Brighton, St Leonards and Blackpool. Some of them did not set out to be quiet and select, but almost always, then as now, this sort of completely new development seems to have had less vigour and liveliness than resorts which grew up round the core of an old town. Blackpool, the earliest of them, was a striking exception to this rule. From the very beginning of its existence, when in the 1750s it was nothing more than a couple of lodging-houses on the edge of a beautiful sandy beach, visitors were remarking on the convivial gusto of the place.

Prices were, from the start, lower than those of any other resort and, as it always has, the town gave its eighteenth-century visitors great value for money. 'The tables,' writes William Hutton, Blackpool's first historian, are supplied 'too well for the price. . . . They excel in cooking; nor is it surprising, for £40 and her maintenance are given to the cook for the season only.' The company were bluff northerners, many of them manufacturers from Bolton or Manchester who were determined to enjoy themselves – 'hysterics and the long train of nervous disorders' were unknown there.

When Dr Granville visited Blackpool in the late 1830s they were still heartily over-eating and many of the people staying in his boarding-house were, he noted, lower down the social scale than those he had met at any other resort. He arrived at Nixon's 'in the nick of time' for dinner. 'We were admitted into a long and lofty apartment having some pretension to the rank of a banquetting-room in which a long, narrow table, groaning under a double line of tin-capped dishes, was awaiting the arrival of the company. A loud scavenger-like bell soon brought the latter, mob-fashion, into the room. . . . Such a motley of honest-looking people – men, women and children (for there were some whose chins did not reach the edge of the table) – it has never been my fortune to meet under the like circumstances in such numbers before – fifty or sixty in all. . . . Methinks the highest in rank here might have been an iron-founder, from near Bradford or Halifax, or a retired wine-merchant from Liverpool. About a dozen chambermaids acted as waiters, and there was not a vestige of man-servant, at which I heartily rejoiced. It fell to my lot to dissect the chickens for the ladies. Abundance of meat and sauce seemed the desirable thing. One whom I had plentifully supplied with leg and pinion and no small portion of the parsley-and-butter, sent soon after to crave for the breast, and a little more of the green sauce! The thing was appalling; and the serious and busy manner in which every hand and mouth

James Burton's design for St Leonards

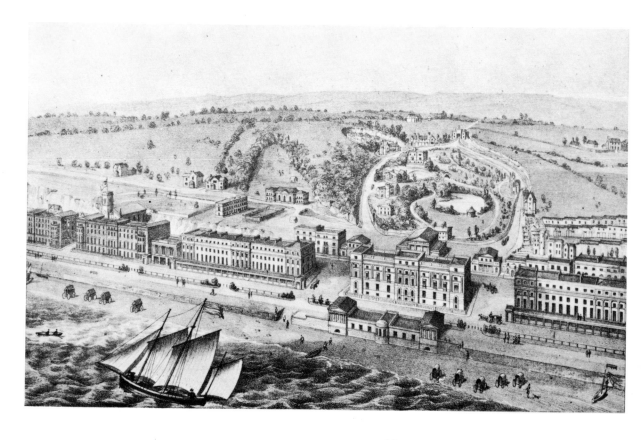

53

seemed to be at work during the first ten minutes, *sans mot dire*, plainly showed how palatable was the fare, and how keenly the sea air and the sea-bathing of Blackpool, had prepared the company for it.'

Compared with Blackpool, most of the other new resorts which Dr Granville visited in the north of England were bleak and dreary. He is scathing about the dullness of New Brighton. It had been founded in the 1830s in wind-swept sandhills near Liverpool. The courage of the man 'who planted the first dwelling-house on such a waste and expected others to follow his example', could only be admired, but, added Dr Granville, 'nothing can equal the air of desolation that prevails around'.

St Leonards was the most elegant completely new seaside town to be built before Queen Victoria came to the throne. It was planned by Sir James Burton in 1828, a mile away from Hastings which was already attracting crowds of summer visitors, including Charles Lamb, who loathed it, and Byron, who enjoyed himself. ('I have been swimming and eating turbot and smuggling neat brandies and silk handkerchiefs . . . and walking on cliffs and tumbling down hills, and making the most of the "dolce far niente" for a fortnight,' wrote Byron from Hastings in 1814.) St Leonards was to have a far more formal and restrained atmosphere than its neighbour.

James Burton designed a charming town with classical terraces overlooking the sea. There was a colonnaded row of shops let only to 'light, genteel trades', a large hotel and elegant assembly rooms. Secluded villas in all the approved, eclectic Regency styles clustered round a public garden laid out in a fashionably informal and romantic manner. Even the toll-gate was made to look like a ruined tower, 'a record of the architect's attention to the picturesque'. 'It was', wrote Dr Granville, 'a little paradise for invalids.'

St Leonards cut itself off from Hastings by placing a large symbolic arch in the road where the two towns met. They should have made incompatible neighbours, but another of the oddities of the history of the seaside is how often a quiet, select resort was to grow up next door to a noisy, crowded one – Frinton and Clacton, Hove and Brighton, Lytham St Anne's and Blackpool – the pattern is repeated again and again, and not only in England. Somehow the proximity seems to suit both parties. It gives everyone the pleasure of having something handy to complain about – either the vulgarity or the snobbery of the goings-on just down the coast.

Continental and American Beginnings

The seaside was not only an invention of the English, it was one of their most successful exports. For centuries Englishmen had been the most enthusiastic travellers in Europe, and they were the first people who thought of bathing at Dieppe and Boulogne or of staying for health and pleasure at Nice – indeed, the south of France might be classed as one of their discoveries.

In the eighteenth century continental doctors, although they enthusiastically recommended hot baths of all sorts, saw no merit whatever in sea-bathing – to them it was another rash, English eccentricity. When Tobias Smollett bathed in Nice in 1763, 'some of the doctors prognosticated immediate death'. Frenchmen retained their distaste for cold water far longer than their English contemporaries and their conversion was slow and reluctant; it was not until the 1830s that they cheerfully began to adopt the English fashion.

The climate, rather than the bathing, brought English visitors flocking to the south of France in the late eighteenth century. Smollett was the first person of influence to praise and publicize it. His book *Travels through France and Italy* – the description of a journey he made in the early 1760s – is full of complaints about the inns, the roads and his health, but he wrote glowingly of Nice in winter and made it sound irresistible to his chilly readers at home. 'When I look around me I can scarce help thinking myself enchanted. The small extent of the country which I see, is all cultivated like a garden . . . full of green trees loaded with oranges, lemons, citrons and bergamots . . . roses, carnations and daffodils blowing in full glory, with such beauty, vigour and perfume as no flower in England ever exhibited. There is less wind and rain in Nice than in any part of the world I know. . . . Such is the serenity of the air, that you see

55

nothing above your head for several months together but a charming blue expanse without cloud or speck.'

When Smollett stayed in Nice it was an impoverished, ancient town. There were no amenities for visitors, for it did not expect any – no library, no music and no furnished apartments to let. But as a direct result of the success of his book its atmosphere began to change. Smollett was a surgeon himself and his views were taken seriously by doctors, and they began to send delicate patients, especially consumptives, on the gruelling sixteen-day journey from London to Nice. Aristocrats, including the Duke of York, one of George III's brothers, followed the invalids and the English visitors began to build themselves villas and create their own social life revolving round the aptly named Hotel d'Angleterre. The fact that Nice was then not part of France but of the Kingdom of Sardinia, a close ally of the British, may also have had something to do with its popularity. By 1786 when Sir James Smith visited the town its attitude to tourists had changed. He was, 'soon disgusted with the gross flattery paid to strangers, and the English in particular. The whole neighbourhood has the air of an English watering-place.'

Every year at the end of April the visitors all packed up and left Nice. Fashionable doctors returned to London and their poor patients were forced to follow them. This extraordinary exodus was caused by the myth that the heat of summer on the Riviera was dangerous and intolerable. 'From the month of May till the beginning of October, the heat is so violent', wrote Smollett, 'that you cannot stir abroad after six in the morning till eight o'clock at night.' Now, this seems nonsense, but perhaps the hot weather would have been too much for eighteenth-century tourists. Decorum glued them to their frock coats and sticky wigs, and plumbing scarcely existed. Throughout the nineteenth century this fear of the Mediterranean summer sun continued, and it was to have an immense influence on the whole pattern of life in the south of France.

After Waterloo, rich English tourists came back to Nice and they also began to settle for the winter in places like Menton and Antibes. Napoleon's new roads made the journey a little shorter, and after having been confined to England by long wars, the thought of carnations blooming in December and of the exclusiveness of the Riviera – for Brighton was getting impossibly crowded – made it seem more desirable then ever.

Soon Nice was crammed every winter with English visitors. There were English hotels, English shops, English newspapers, English churches and 'quantities of gossip and a great deal of dressiness'. The Promenade des Anglais is the grandest monument to the influence of the English on the Riviera. It was begun in 1830 at the suggestion of an Anglican clergyman to provide work for the local unemployed, and though it was inspired by the promenades which were then beginning to be built along the edge of the sea at many English resorts, it ultimately became far more spectacular than any of them. By the 1850s it was thronged every afternoon with splendid carriages, and they often contained Russian grand dukes or German princesses, for by then Nice was becoming a magnet for international rather than just English high society.

Cannes, however, in the mid-nineteenth century was still completely dominated by English visitors. It had been a small village when Lord Brougham, the great Whig orator and Lord Chancellor, built himself a house there in the 1830s. He persuaded King Louis-Philippe to grant the funds to construct its fine harbour, and it was his long attachment to the place that turned it into a favourite English colony – fashionable but not flashy. 'The society of Cannes is very pleasant – so simple and kindly without formality or overdressing,' wrote Miss Margaret Maria Brewster, a rather prim Scottish lady in poor health, who was typical of the sort of people who stayed there in the 1840s and 1850s. She found the air, 'like drinking champagne . . . rather *too* exciting', but enjoyed visiting the 'very pretty little English church built by Mr. Woolfield', taking tea and being shown stuffed snakes by Lord Brougham, discussing the fatiguing business of constantly having to shake hands with the servants and the horrors of the mosquitoes. 'You have no idea of the social weight of mosquitoes. In the morning it is the subject of general conversation.' She makes Cannes sound like an isolated outpost of the Empire, and even developed the habit of distributing to the natives Calvinist tracts translated into the local patois.

Before the middle of the nineteenth century, the Channel ports, while retaining their old functions, had also become seaside resorts. Dieppe, Boulogne and Calais had long been the most familiar towns in France to British tourists. Here the English gained their first and last impressions of the Continent and by the eighteenth century the French were sometimes prepared to modify their habits to fit in with English tastes; the hotels could be induced to cook chops, and even the beggar boys knew a few useful English phrases. However, it took the natives of Dieppe and Boulogne many years to realize the possibilities of the fashion of sea-bathing. Some travellers, including the intrepid Smollett, had bathed at Boulogne in spite of the complete lack of amenities, and in 1808 the Comtesse de Boigne, one of the first grand Frenchwomen to adopt the English habit in her own country, took the plunge several times at Dieppe. She

The casino at Dieppe by Leprince after Ulrich, 1822. From *Excursions sur les Côtes et dans les Ports de Normandie*

was followed about by large giggling crowds and nicknamed 'l'Anglaise', which must have been discouraging.

There was a great increase in the number of English tourists passing through the channel ports after the end of the Napoleonic wars; one of them, the painter Benjamin Robert Haydon, commented neatly on the contrast between Brighton's fine new terraces overlooking the water and the old-fashioned layout of Dieppe: 'Dieppe turns its back upon the sea, as if in disgust at the sight of an element on which her country has always been beaten.'

Astute businessmen in Dieppe finally realized that it would be worth improving the bathing arrangements and by 1822 the sea-front, which had long served as a municipal rubbish dump, had been cleared up and a charming classical casino opened. Its functions combined those of an English marine library and bathing-rooms. It hired out bathing-dresses and had rooms for billiards, reading, dancing and cards. There were no bathing-machines – the beach was too steep for them – but little striped tents to undress in. The French equivalent of the dippers, the *guide-baigneurs*, patrolled the beach in striped jerseys and leather hats and did very good business, for police regulations had been passed making it illegal to bathe without one of them in attendance.

A member of the French royal family first took to sea-bathing in 1824. Marie-Caroline, Duchesse de Berri, caused a great stir when she arrived in Dieppe. She eagerly adopted every seaside pastime, dancing all night at the casino, which was re-named the Bains Caroline in her honour, going for trips in rowing-boats in rough weather, presiding over fêtes and concerts. For five summers she kept returning to the town, bringing many gay and fashionable visitors in her wake. She even enjoyed bathing. The citizens of Dieppe had not yet quite worked out the etiquette of conducting a royal personage into the sea.

58

She was accompanied on her first bathe of the season by a doctor, immaculately dressed for attending a princess. He offered her a white-gloved hand and, as if they were about to open a ball, formally escorted her deep into the water. 'C'était à mourir de rire,' wrote an observer.

By 1830, when revolution put Louis-Philippe on the throne and the Duchesse de Berri was sent into exile, Dieppe had become established with the French as well as the English as a seaside resort. Though its patroness had vanished, the bathing, the music and the gaiety made more and more fashionable people visit the town. At last the conversion of the French to the seaside had really begun.

In the next two decades other places on the north coast of France, Dinard for instance, began to attract visitors. Most of them were originally discovered by artists or writers looking for picturesque, cheap villages in which to spend the summer working. When Alexandre Dumas went to Trouville it was still just a few fishermen's cottages in a charming valley. His description of its beauties – he predictably compares the fascination of the sea to that of a beloved mistress – and the excellent, cheap food – on his first night he dined, for a tiny sum, on soup, lamb cutlets, sole, lobster mayonnaise, roast snipe and a shrimp salad – must have impressed many of his readers. By the 1850s Trouville had become a seaside resort more or less on the English pattern. The visits of the

The Empress Eugénie at Trouville, Boudin, 1863

Empress Eugénie confirmed its popularity and made it even more fashionable than Dieppe.

By then, too, Ostend and Blankenberghe had also become flourishing resorts with casinos and bathing-machines and quantities of English visitors. When Jules Janni described the scene at Ostend in 1833, it seemed to him that most of the people who patronized it were hideous English invalids. He is most scathing about their appearance in the water: 'C'est un atroce spectacle.'

In other parts of Europe in the first half of the nineteenth century people were also beginning to stay by the sea. An earnest interest in their health seems to have been the most important motive in bringing them to the coast, and the new resorts in places like Holland and Russia sound deadly dull. Dr Granville describes Scheveningen in The Hague. 'Here in 1836, I beheld invalids who had come from distant

The happy effects of continental mixed bathing, c. 1860

Avant.   Pendant.   Après.

parts of Germany for the benefit of sea-water and who were dying of ennui.'

The Russians also became over-enthusiastic followers of Dr Russell and rigorous sea-bathing was prescribed for almost every illness – including chills caught from too much bathing. A minimum of fifty immersions was considered essential, but patients were encouraged to take 'The Larger Cure' of sixty or seventy. The aristocratic Russian invalids who visited the Black Sea coast kept strict accounts of the number of bathes they had had by making chalk marks on the walls of their huts every time they came out of the sea, 'red as a crab, dripping with sea-water and trembling all over with cold'.

In Colonial America the roads were so poor and the centres of population were so scattered that it was inconceivable that there should be much travelling for pleasure. A few people who lived by the sea, like a Mr Reuben Tucker of Long Beach, turned their homes into boarding-houses for 'the health and entertainment of pleasure seekers', but in the eighteenth century there was only one place that could be called a seaside resort. This was Newport, Rhode Island, which was then at the height of its prosperity as a port. In the 1760s rich planters from the South and the West Indies used to leave their estates in the summer to escape from the hot weather, and sail to Newport for a month or two of cool breezes and good society. They were a very small *élite*. The social column of the *Newport Mercury* lists only about 400 visitors between 1767 and 1775. Their amusements sound almost exactly the same as those at far away Scarborough – racing on horseback across the sands, dancing in the open air, playing cards in the 'long room' – and they were, no doubt, consciously following the fashion set by their English relations. Only their excursions to Goat Island for huge turtle dinners strike an exotic and specifically American note. In 1762 a company of actors had arrived in Newport and for two or three nights plays were added to the diversions, but the performance of *Othello* so shocked the Rhode Island Assembly that they imposed a crippling fine of £100 per actor if any of them should dare to perform there in public again.

This puritanism, which had a very strong influence on American social life, especially in the North, was reinforced by the Revolution, and at the beginning of the nineteenth century many European travellers complained that Americans had become so absorbed in hard work and making money that they had quite lost all talent for enjoying themselves. It was not an atmosphere in which fashionable watering-place amusements could flourish, and Newport, which had been badly affected by the war, went into temporary decline as a resort. In a more easy-going, informal style, however, visits to the seaside continued. A few places on the East Coast, which could be reached by boat and stagecoach from New York and Philadelphia, Cape May and Long Branch in New Jersey, for instance, began to attract summer visitors. They generally stayed not in furnished apartments or inns, but in big, primitive boarding-houses. The grand-sounding Atlantic Hotel at Cape May was, in 1810, nothing but a huge barn divided at night by a sheet – the men slept on one side of it and the women on the other. In 1805 there were three wood-frame boarding-houses at Long Branch, each of which could house a hundred guests. Their scale was uniquely American – the biggest boarding-house in which Dr Granville stayed when he toured the English watering-places in the late 1830s was Nixon's at Blackpool, where fifty or sixty people sat down to dinner, but this was an exception; there were few hotels in England at the beginning of the nineteenth century which catered for as many as a hundred guests.

The amusements of the people who stayed in these boarding-

On the Bluff at Long Branch at the Bathing Hour. A wood engraving by Winslow Homer for *Harper's Weekly*, 1870

houses were as basic as the crude, whitewashed buildings themselves. They ate well, fish and oysters being the specialities – in one Long Branch boarding-house guests could help themselves from a heap of oysters under the shed – but time often passed slowly. The chief excitement was meeting new people, and the arrival of the weekly boat from New York or Philadelphia was eagerly awaited; though sometimes strait-laced newcomers brought the impromptu entertainments, like dancing and dominoes, to a halt.

By the 1850s there had been a thorough revival of frivolity in America; visiting Long Branch and especially Cape May had become the fashion, and Newport was once more a select resort. Many of the visitors who thronged these seaside towns came from the South. Before the Civil War about fifty thousand Southerners used to come north on pleasure trips every summer; a lot of them went to take the waters at the famous inland spa Saratoga Springs, but many Southern belles became the toast of Cape May or Newport.

The boarding-houses had been eclipsed by enormous hotels round which social life revolved. The Mount Vernon at Cape May had a dining-room large enough for 750 people to be served at once. Dancing and cards were no longer frowned on; gambling clubs had become part of American resort life, and in the evenings the dining-rooms of the big hotels were cleared and everyone waltzed enthusiastically or did the 'Cape May Polka'.

All along the Atlantic coast from Maine to New Jersey, small fishing villages began to be discovered and adopted by a few city families. As in France, some of the most beautiful places which later became resorts of the rich were first discovered by artists and writers. Thomas Cole was delighted with the spectacular mountain and ocean scenery of Bar Harbour in Maine when he went there in 1844. 'It is not pure Norway, it is Norway and Italy combined,' cried one of his followers, and soon New York businessmen with artistic wives were going there to see it for themselves.

There was a uniquely American and quite unfrivolous form of seaside resort which flourished in the mid-nineteenth century. These seaside settlements developed out of the big religious camp meetings which had long been a feature of American life. Crowds of fervent settlers used to gather for weeks at a time to sing hymns, give their testimonies and live in tents. From about the 1830s isolated coastal sites began to be found for these camps so that the more innocent seaside pleasures could be combined with all the religious intensity. One of the earliest was started in 1835, when a group of Methodists pitched their tents in a

grove of scrub oaks at Oak Bluffs on Martha's Vineyard. Very gradually the tents were converted into wooden cottages built on almost exactly the same lines – one year board walls would replace canvas ones, and the next, perhaps, a porch would be added until finally the tent had been completely replaced by a little tent-shaped gingerbread Gothic house.

Ocean Grove and Ocean City in New Jersey also began as Methodist encampments, and many of their visitors were still living under canvas at the turn of the century. There were severe restrictions at all the religious resorts – no liquor, no entertainers or buskers, no swearing and, on the Sabbath, no bathing, boating or driving – but they thrived and long retained their peculiar, exclusive character. The idea of a seaside tent city was later adopted as a cheap form of holiday accommodation without accompanying religious restrictions.

Americans had taken to the seaside with unselfconscious delight. Whether they spent their evenings praying or dancing, there was, 'no end of watery joy till the dinner bell rings'. Bathing never seems to have been surrounded by quite all the medical myths and crazy etiquette that were attached to it on the other side of the Atlantic; no doubt it did one good, but mainly it was just a natural and amusing way of passing the time on a hot day. There was a simplicity about the American approach that makes all the ritual involved in getting an Englishman into the water seem odder than ever.

Bathing-machines never became general, perhaps the heavy swell on the East Coast and the fact that the tide does not usually go out far, made them unsuitable. People generally changed in communal huts on the shore and wore odd combinations of old clothes rather than special bathing-gowns. Dippers do not seem to have existed. There is an intriguing description of alternative bathing customs at Long Branch in the 1830s in *Domestic Manners of the Americans* the famous, waspish book by Frances Trollope, Anthony's mother.

'Many of the best families had left the city [Philadelphia] for different watering-places, and others were daily following. Long Branch is the fashionable bathing-place on the Jersey shore, to which many resort both from this place and from New York; the description given of the manner of bathing appeared to me rather extraordinary, but the account was confirmed by so many different people, that I could not doubt its correctness. The shore, it seems, is too bold to admit of bathing-machines and the ladies have therefore recourse to another mode of ensuring the enjoyment of sea-bathing with safety. The accommodation at Long Branch is almost entirely at large boarding-houses, where all

65

The Bathe at Newport.
American mixed bathing.
A wood engraving by
Winslow Homer from
Harper's Weekly, 1858

the company live at a table d'hôte. It is customary for ladies on arriving to look round among the married gentlemen, the first time they meet at table, and to select the one her fancy leads her to prefer as a protector in her purposed visit to the realms of Neptune; she makes her request, which is always graciously received, that he would lead her to taste the briny wave; but another fair one must select the same protector, else the arrangement cannot be complete as custom does not authorise *tête-à-tête* immersions.'

By the 1850s mixed bathing without all these elaborate excuses was in full swing. At Newport parties of ladies and gentlemen dashed 'hand in hand, sometimes forty of them together into the surf'. The men 'handed about their pretty partners as if they were dancing quadrilles'. English visitors were shocked, but by then England was alone in rigidly segregating the sexes in the sea. At most continental resorts half the pleasure of the seaside was in watery flirtations. At Trouville and Ostend the ladies bathed holding their parasols above their heads and 'never unaccompanied by gentlemen escorts'. But at isolated places along the New Jersey coast even wilder things were going on. After they had changed their clothes on the sands, the men from Ryan's boarding-house at Absecon Beach carried 'blushing and screaming maidens' up to the top of the sandhills, and then tied their feet together and with much hilarity rolled them down into the water. Their contemporaries at Cromer would have found the scene appalling and scarcely credible.

The Family Holiday

'The little people are in their glory here,' wrote Richard Doyle in an article in *The Cornhill Magazine* in 1861. 'The sands have surely been made for them. . . . What intense happiness to dabble up to their ankles in the sea! What delight to dig canals with little spades, and to build up great castles in the sand! What fun to bury one another, and how jolly to dig one another up again, and what a gratification to spoil one another's clothes.' It seems a timeless scene, but in fact that description could scarcely have been written sixty years before. It was the Victorians who realized what a paradise the beach was for children and how long and happily they could be amused by sand and water. Those little wooden spades had first been thought of by Rousseau as improving tools for infant gardening; English parents started to buy them for their children at the end of the eighteenth century, but it was not until the Victorian age began that they became essential seaside equipment. Miniature buckets were not yet as common – but top hats inadvertently put down on the beach were excellent for making sandpies; and there were small wooden wheelbarrows for carting sand about.

Victorian parents seem to have been surprisingly prepared to allow their overdressed children, wearing layer after layer of starched and frilly clothes, to get deliciously wet and sandy. There is a cartoon by John Leech, who drew innumerable seaside scenes for *Punch*, headed *Real Enjoyment* which shows a mother and an ecstatic little boy. '*Charley* (who is wet through for the 9th time) – Oh Ma! We've been so jolly! We've been filling one another's hair with sand and making boats of our boots and having such fun.' It was all part of the pleasures and frustrations of a new institution – the family holiday.

Children could play little part in the regulated spa-like

amusements at seaside watering-places of the eighteenth century and the Regency. Usually it did not occur to their parents to think of bringing them – they were left behind at home with the servants. If their health required a visit to the sea, they were generally expected to behave like miniature adults. They were not encouraged to hang about on the beach after their early morning bathe, but had to amuse themselves unobtrusively in the grown-up settings of the marine library or the assembly rooms – there are several children, and even one or two dogs, behaving quite decorously in the late-eighteenth-century engraving of Hall's Library at Margate.

Ramsgate Sands by
Arthur Boyd Houghton,
1861

By the 1840s it had become a middle-class fashion to idealize big families and cosy domesticity. The early Victorians had absorbed the Romantic theories which attached a special value to the innocence of childhood; and though they were appallingly blind to the sufferings of the children of the poor, and may sometimes have treated their own children with alternating sentimentality and harshness, they were generally far more sympathetic to their special needs, far more willing to consider their children's pleasure as well as their own, than previous generations had been.

The Queen and Prince Albert set a splendid example in domesticity, and they soon became devotees of the family seaside holiday. Queen Victoria disliked Brighton. The crowds there pestered and annoyed her. 'The people are very indiscreet and troublesome here,' she wrote, 'really the place is quite a prison.' The town crowded too closely round the Pavilion, it was, 'impossible to catch more than a glimpse of the sea from the upper windows'; and as she had more and more children, it began to seem too small, as well as utterly alien to her own and Albert's taste in decoration. In

At the Seaside by Richard Doyle. From *The Cornhill Magazine*, 1861

1846 the Queen moved to her own new seaside house at Osborne on the Isle of Wight – 'our dear little Home'. She rebuilt it as an Italian palace and the nearby towns, Ryde and Ventnor, prospered. While Albert amused himself laying out the grounds, she sat snugly in a semicircular beach hut which he had designed for her, watching the children play on the beach, or they all 'plunged about' in the sea or went shell-collecting. 'How happy we are here!' she wrote. 'And never do I enjoy myself more peacefully than when I can be so much with my beloved Albert and follow him everywhere.'

Many well-off people chose a secluded resort, as the royal family had done, and bought or rented houses there to which they returned surrounded by their relations, summer after summer. Cromer, for example, was, until the 1870s dominated by a group of rich, philanthropic, interrelated families – the Gurneys, Hoares, Buxtons and Barclays. This great clan of cousins amused themselves together riding, swimming, picnicking and doing good works. 'It was an entirely family party,' wrote Ellen Buxton from Cromer in 1863, '33 in all.'

Professional men were now prepared to spend their summer vacations taking their whole families to the seaside. The house in town was shut up for a month or so, or looked after by a respectable elderly female, while the paterfamilias, his wife and children with governesses and nurse-maids went to stay in a rented apartment in a seaside resort. It also began to be common for city businessmen to become temporary commuters in the summer, taking the train to London every morning from resorts like Brighton or Eastbourne while their families stayed by the sea.

The big middle-class Victorian families, with all their cousins and hangers-on, were self-sufficient enough not to miss much of the unified social life which had been a feature of resort life for earlier generations; for by the 1840s all the distinctive spa-like institutions, which had both controlled the conduct of visitors and served to introduce them to each other, were rapidly declining. The well-known seaside resorts were now too crowded for the old spa system, based on the pattern of eighteenth-century Bath with its small *élite* clientele, to survive.

The office of Master of Ceremonies at Brighton was already practically defunct when it was finally suppressed in 1855. In some fashionable resorts 'presentable people' still continued to find that morning calls 'added to a sojourn at the seaside, render the place very desirable'. At Brighton in the 1860s, the local newspaper still listed the grandest new arrivals, but did not give 'a complete directory of its floating population', and most people now seem only to have called on families they already knew at home.

The marine libraries still survived – in fact, even the smallest seaside town claimed to have one, even if it consisted only of a couple of shelves of unsuitable books beside the counter in the general store – they were, however, no longer quite the social centres they had been in the eighteenth century, though they were still 'very peculiar places'.

Bathing-rooms were disappearing, though there was still one at Margate in the 1850s, 'fitted out with every luxury including yesterday's newspaper and a piano with a rich banjo tone'. Now every morning there was a race to reserve the bathing-machines, young ladies picked up their skirts and dashed down the esplanade to where the machines stood, sometimes three or four deep at the edge of the sea. There were more of them than ever – damp and musty inside and crawling with earwigs, with wet bits of carpet on the floor, and broken mirrors on the walls. They shook and bumped horribly as they lumbered into the sea, but now they were sometimes parked in the water for most of the day and approached by a rickety drawbridge of planks which grew longer, and more challenging to negotiate in a crinoline, as the tide came up.

The bathing-women remained until the 1860s when they began to be replaced by stout ropes attached to the machines. They are still always depicted as old, bonneted ogres and always referred to in songs and cartoons as Martha in memory of Martha Gunn. Their fixed smiles and commanding cry, 'Come on, little fellow!' struck fear into many a young Victorian heart.

The spa amusements were fading, but the piers, winter gardens, amusement parks, tennis courts, cricket grounds and concert halls which were to replace them in the last decades of the century had not yet come into their own; now everything happened on the beach. Led by the children, all the visitors, and everyone who hoped to make money out of entertaining them, flocked down on to the shore. When the weather was fine, the sands of every popular Victorian resort became noisy, gay and marvellously animated, but when it was wet, the English seaside in the mid-nineteenth century must have been quite dismal – worse even than it is now. There is a cartoon by Leech that sums up the awful boredom of a rainy day by the sea. It shows a young man staring blankly out of his hotel window and wondering if 'perhaps stropping his razors might amuse him'.

But the sun often did shine, and here is a list of some of the things that were happening on a fine day on Brighton beach in the 1860s. The quotation is from a book by Cuthbert Bede called *Mattins and Muttons* which was published in 1866 – it is a fascinating description of a holiday in Brighton, thinly disguised as a novel.

'Crowds of children – ringing music of the town band – further on a string band, Punch and Judy – man who sang comic songs, highland dancers, acrobat with two sons, foreigner with performing canaries, performing pony called "the horse of sensibility" whose feats of spelling and fortune-telling would put to shame many of the little boys who looked on. Performing monkeys, musical glasses and bells, sellers of fruits, cakes and gingerbreads, a man with a bundle of balloonlike balls of various colours, a man with a fez who sings "Brandy balls! Who'll buy my brandy balls?" Sellers of bouquets, violets, shell-boxes, pincushions made of cow's hooves, lace and embroidery, watch chains, dogs, newspapers.'

There were innumerable entertainers and pedlars in Victorian England who normally made a living performing in the city streets and parks, at fairs and race meetings. In the summer they followed their customers to the seaside to amuse the captive audience on the sands, and they gave a peculiarly urban quality to the beaches.

Cuthbert Bede leaves out three of the most typical Victorian beach entertainers – the nigger minstrels, the German bands and the organ-grinders. The nigger minstrels were an essential part of the English seaside scene in the second half of the nineteenth century, and they were its first import from America. Black-faced comedians and singers began to be popular there in the early 1830s, and in the next ten years the form of the minstrel show evolved and became an American institution. In 1843 the first American minstrel troupe appeared in London and later the show put on by the Moore and Burgess Minstrels ran for decades. Their success encouraged many smaller troupes to cross the Atlantic and led to innumerable English imitations. The minstrel shows, which needed no scenery, could easily be performed on the sands, and they were perfect for the seaside family audience. The all-male troupes, with their baggy pants, bow ties, and blackened faces, used to stand in a semicircle on the shore playing their cornets, concertinas, tambourines, 'bones' and banjos – an instrument new to England which they made immensely popular. (Singing minstrel songs and accompanying oneself on the banjo brought back happy memories in the long winter evenings.)

The shows had a fixed formula, mixing riddles, songs like *Polly-Wolly Doodle* and *Swanee River*, and good, clean jokes. A grave, white-faced compère, 'Mr Interlocutor' always stood in the centre of the group, and was the butt of the comic 'Corner Men'. At the seaside they developed a great rapport with their audience, especially the children.

72

Nigger minstrels on
Brighton beach, *c.* 1870

Minstrel 'uncles', 'Uncle Bones' or 'Uncle Mack' used to organize children's singing and dancing competitions and give impressive displays of remembering their names from one year to another – for next summer they were sure to meet again on the sands. In a very short time the nigger minstrels had made themselves as much a part of the seaside as shrimps and bathing-machines.

The German bands, wearing fancy uniforms and tootling loudly on a variety of wind instruments, were a familiar sight in every mid-Victorian town and provided much of the bouncy seaside background music. They were originally Bavarians who came to England in the spring and returned home to their farms in the autumn, but towards the end of the

73

century the name German band was given to almost any small group of wandering professional musicians. By then, however, they were being eclipsed at the resorts by big amateur brass bands who played on splendid new iron bandstands.

The quantities of barrel-organs at the seaside seem to have had a particularly exasperating effect on people – at Brighton, the mayor was persuaded to ban them early in the 1860s – and sometimes the noise was not exhilarating, but awful, especially as all the conflicting musicians took to the streets in the early morning before the beach became crowded and strummed and bawled outside hotel windows. Victorian letters, cartoons and novels are full of groans about seaside noise. 'Indeed, noise seems to be the grand joy in life,' wrote Jane Welsh Carlyle from Ramsgate in 1861. 'A brass band plays all through our breakfast, and repeats the performance often during the day, and the brass band is

A GREAT PLAGUE IN LIFE.

PATERFAMILIAS, WHOSE PET AVERSION IS STREET MUSIC, GOES TO THE SEA-SIDE, HOPING TO ESCAPE FROM THE NUISANCE, HE IS AT BREAKFAST,—BEAUTIFUL VIEW, NEW-LAID EGG, &C., &C.—WHEN—

OH, HORROR!

Cartoon for *Punch* by
John Leech, *c.* 1860

succeeded by a band of Ethiopians, and that again by a band of female fiddlers! and interspersed with these are individual barrel-organs, individual Scotch bagpipes, individual French horns!' (She did not much care for Ramsgate, and also complained about the smells. 'The smells are nasty! Spoiled shrimps complicated with cesspool.')

And Cuthbert Bede gives a description of the sounds which, as well as the cries of newsboys, fisherwomen and oyster vendors, greeted the Melladew family in *Mattins and*

74

Muttons when they came down to breakfast on the first morning of their holiday in a rented apartment in Brighton.

'A brass band in the next street could be very plainly heard through the back window of their inner room rousing tumultuous echoes with the soldiers' chorus in Faust; and just as they had changed that air for another that was, if possible, more noisy and clamorous, the unmelodious howling and thrumming of a nigger band stationed under their bow window assailed their ears on the other side with a wish to be in Dixie – a wish that Mrs. Melladew earnestly hoped might be instantly fulfilled to the singers.'

When one had bathed and grown tired of the musicians and trinket-sellers, the beach still held many other diversions. The special pleasure of lazily reading a novel with the sound of the sea in one's ears was a Victorian discovery. The books and newspapers which used to be read only in the marine library, or in one's rooms, were now taken down on to the sands. 'To sit against a boat and read a novel and do fancy work is an accredited method among young ladies to pass the noontide hours.'

'The only place where I really relish a book is the seaside,' reflected Mrs Caudle. 'The ocean always seems to me to open the mind. . . . Sometimes at the seaside – especially when the tide's down – I feel so happy; quite as if I could cry.'

When one's book grew boring, one could sketch the fishing boats, the rock formations and the waves, or go for a sail in a pleasure boat. 'The "Victoria and Albert", the "Empress Eugenie", the "Wedding Ring", the "Honeymoon", and the "John and Nancy" – all the gay, white-sailed, party-coloured boats pushed away from the shore with many giggling groups who thought they could never be sick on such a smooth sea.'

Or one could ride a hired hack, or drive one's carriage along the shore with its wheels splashing in the waves. Every sizeable Victorian resort had stables with quantities of horses and ponies for hire at rates which the holidaymakers complained were far higher than those in town. Ellen Buxton, who had a pony of her own at the seaside, describes in her childhood journal the pleasures and surprises of a family ride on the sands at Cromer in 1862.

'On Wednesday afternoon we took a most delishous ride on the shore, it was quite low tide and the ponies were very good. They did not mind the sea in the least, it was the first time that Star and Derry had ever been on the shore but they did not mind it in the least. . . . As we were riding home, Alfred was galloping through a rather large and deep pool (such as often come on the shore) – when that wicked little beast Derry, going at full gallop stopped short in the very middle and sent Alfred over his head, head

Crowded pleasure boats at
Ramsgate

first and legs up into the water, he went *entirely under* the
water and was of course drenched through to the skin. . . .
Each time the boys fall off their ponies, my Father gives them
sixpence.'

There were donkeys, too, for the children, though
sometimes young ladies still rode them as they had in
Brighton in the Regency – they looked very odd from
behind with their crinolines all bunched up to their shoulders.
Miniature carriages pulled by goats were a seaside speciality;
'little landaus, phaetons and wagonettes drawn by one or
two goats and filled with little ladies and gentlemen
dressed in the height of fashion'.

Apart from riding and driving, there were few beach sports. Croquet, however, was sometimes played on the sands, and men who had the insatiable Victorian urge to be always shooting at something could, in the absence of pheasants or stags, take pot-shots at the seagulls. 'The saucy gulls hovered and dipped, hovered and dipped regardless of the pop pop popping from the gang of unsteady-handed sportsmen in the boats.'

One could still flirt discreetly; for in spite of the fact that it was now so much more difficult to be formally introduced to new people at the seaside, and that the sexes were segregated in the water, resorts were still great places for flirting. There lingered about the beaches subdued traces of that jolly sexiness that had been so much part of their atmosphere in the eighteenth century. Crinolines billowed in the wind revealing distracting amounts of ankle, melting eyes gazed over library books, interesting messages were written in the sand with the tips of canes and parasols, and determined young people even contrived to get cut off by the tide. 'It's the worst of these watering-places,' cries one of Leech's plain spinsters. 'There are so many adventurers on the look out for wives that one is always in fear of being proposed to.'

At the seaside the demure façade of well-brought-up Victorian girls sometimes slipped. In the *Illustrated Times* of 1856 there is a description of two of them at a concert

Weston Sands 1864 by H. Hopkins and Edmund Havell

77

Mermaids combing their enticing locks by Richard Doyle. From *The Cornhill Magazine*, 1861

in the Marine Library at Margate. 'There were two naughty, but extremely interesting young ladies in cavalier hats with lavender strings who kept laughing all the time the lady sang. They held their handkerchiefs up to their mouths, but their eyes were all screwed up with giggling and they kept glancing slyly at one another. The sea air has an awful effect on young girls or they would not have done so.'

On every beach there were still old men with telescopes, but now they usually trained them on the ships on the horizon. It needed courage to defy the prevailing prudishness and peer openly at the girls in the sea, besides it was hardly worth it. Mid-Victorian descriptions of the seaside are full of comments on how unattractive they looked. (Leech found them a charming sight, but Cuthbert Bede accuses him of flattering his 'mermaids'. They made 'such pretty studies for the unsurpassed pencil of Leech', but their 'bedraggled forms, bobbing up and down in the shallow water, look so far from enchanting to the eye of dull reality.') Their ragged blue bathing-gowns which were usually hired with the machines seem to have been peculiarly unbecoming.

It was when the girls were dressed again, but still had their damp hair, 'which requires drying, you know, after having been in the sea – streaming about their shoulders, and in the wind, in the most picturesque and bewitching way', that the excitement began. In no other public place would Victorian girls have been seen with their long hair flowing wild and loose – it was always tied back into buns or nets, or tortured into ringlets. Letting one's hair down had the most intimate associations – no wonder it 'made the men stare so' on the beach. In America this mild seaside fetish went a little further. At Cape May in the 1850s a girl's popularity was assessed by the number of beaux crowding round her waiting for a turn to brush her wet hair.

When reading, listening, sketching and even flirting palled, one could always just sit and gaze at the sea. The chairs which were used for all this sitting about are, to our eyes, one of the oddest features of Victorian beach scenes. They are ordinary dining-room or bedroom chairs which look extremely bizarre in their new sandy setting. In the *Illustrated Times* article mentioned above there is a description of how they got on to the beach. In the early morning at Margate 'the old women were just bringing out their chairs and ranging them in rows "against the bathing company should arrive". What strange rickety old bits of painted wood and cane work those chairs were, for so many to get a good living out of. . . . All had lost their varnish and paint and turned as grey as lichens. There were bedroom chairs with the rushes worn away and discarded drawing-room chairs with a few bits of gilding still on them, and bamboo chairs from foreign parts and kitchen chairs with hard wooden seats. The sands are the knacker's yard for chairs; and when they are too old and seedy to be worth houseroom they are packed off to Mrs. Brown or Mrs. Smith or some other famous charwoman – she will turn them to account so long as nails and string will hold together.'

There are many of these discarded chairs, one with its legs almost in the water, in Frith's *Ramsgate Sands*, a picture which rather ponderously includes all the most characteristic elements of a mid-nineteenth-century beach. The children, the nigger minstrels, the donkeys, the Punch and Judy man, the boatmen and the trinket-sellers are all there, and Frith captures the domesticated, middle-class atmosphere of a typical resort of the early 1850s.

The painting is full of telling details, for example, in spite of the grey English weather, most of Frith's ladies have taken their parasols – essential seaside accessories all through the nineteenth century – down on to the sands. Many of them are also protecting their hands with gloves, and even the little girls are wearing bonnets with extraordinary contraptions attached to their brims, which could be pulled down to shield their complexions from every dangerous ray of the sun – they looked, as Leech noted, like miniature bathing-machine canopies. These odd attachments were

Life at the Seaside (Ramsgate Sands) by W. P. Frith. The painting was begun in 1852 from sketches made at Ramsgate in 1851. It was bought for Queen Victoria on private view day at the Royal Academy for 1,000 guineas. Reproduced by Gracious Permission of H.M. the Queen

known as 'uglies' and were popular at the seaside in the late forties and early fifties when nineteenth-century female sun-phobia was at its height.

Ramsgate Sands was the first of the minutely detailed panoramas of contemporary life that made Frith's name and were a quite new departure in English painting; and it inspired many other English artists to paint the seaside in the 1860s. The shore was a shrewd choice of subject with which to begin his series of modern scenes. The crowded sands were indeed an essentially modern sight – as new and as full of incident as the great railway terminus which was to be the subject of one of his later pictures.

The railways, of course, had an immense effect on the English seaside. They were essential to the spread of the middle-class family holiday, and in the long run they played a crucial part in making a visit to the seaside hugely popular with all classes.

In the 1830s railway mania had begun to sweep the country. The network of lines which was to criss-cross Victorian England was being mapped out, and many of the tracks connecting the main centres of industry and population had already been built. It did not take long for the local worthies at most prominent seaside resorts to realize how much railway connections would increase their prosperity, and many of them began to petition the railway companies and parliament with their claims.

There was great municipal rejoicing when, after decades of planning and persuasion, the London to Brighton line was finally opened in 1841. The first train was greeted with bands, banquets, fireworks and huge crowds. 'Parties of ladies and gentlemen were formed on every brow; and every field and meadow from Preston to Withdean and Patcham had its mass of human life. . . . At about twenty minutes after twelve the approach of the train was announced to those from whose sight it was yet hid by a thousand cries of "Here they come".'

Once a seaside town had acquired a station and a line connecting it with London or another great centre of population, there was always an immediate increase in the number of its visitors, and as more and more holidaymakers arrived the resorts swelled to accommodate them – the first new area to be built up was always around the station, which was usually on the outskirts of the town. Brighton, which was already booming, grew at a greatly increased rate after the coming of the railway. Between 1831 and 1841 only 437 new houses were built there and many of them stood empty, but in the first ten years after the line had been opened, 2,806 new houses sprang up. The rapid growth of many resorts, Southend, for example, and in the north, Southport and Blackpool, dates from the opening of direct railway communications, and seaside towns like Bournemouth and Cromer which delayed in establishing them remained, for the time being, small.

Some resorts, which had once been fashionable, declined sharply because they were by-passed by the railway. In the 1850s, a rented apartment could be had at Sidmouth for the summer at half the price which a similar one would have cost at Teignmouth. People were put off visiting Sidmouth by the long coach journey from Exeter, while at Teignmouth there was a convenient new station. Cornwall, without railways and with bad roads, long remained wild and deserted, only visited by intrepid searchers after the picturesque – Wilkie Collins gave his description of a walking tour there in the 1850s the graphic title *Rambles Beyond Railways*.

There were many rival railway companies in mid-Victorian England, and the ones which controlled the lines that took passengers to the sea soon began to have a proprietorial interest in the particular stretch of coast which they served. Later in the century a company sometimes even undertook to develop a resort in order to provide passengers for its trains. The pier, promenade and public gardens at Cleethorpes in Lincolnshire, for example, were all financed by an enterprising local railway company.

In spite of all the advantages that a railway line brought to a seaside resort, there was usually some local opposition to be overcome before one could be opened. A man jumped up at a Bournemouth public meeting and launched into rhyme.

'Tis well from far to hear the railway scream
And watch the curling, lingering clouds of steam;
But let not Bournemouth – health's approved abode,
Court the near presence of the iron road.

Many people in the early days of the railways considered that trains were a particularly unsuitable and dangerous form of transport for the invalids on whom many seaside resorts depended for much of their custom. Dr Granville describes these hypersensitive objections. 'What, if a person is endowed with such exquisite sensibility of the nervous system that the clumsy slamming of a door by a careless foot-man at home, or the tumbling down of a set of fireirons, at once produces a start, a commotion and a headache for a day? Can such a person trust himself to railway travelling . . . can he risk a rapid journey in one of the locomotives of the Western or South Western trains, to rattle on at the rate of thirty miles an hour?' Rail travel was accused of producing 'apoplexy' and – 'the sudden plunging into the darkness of a tunnel cannot fail to make work for occulists'; but gradually, in spite of a series of bad accidents, these fears subsided, and by the 1850s the railways were generally accepted as a quick and convenient way of travelling.

There were other more realistic objections. Everyone connected with coaching feared that the railways would kill off long-distance road travel, and they were right. Before the end of the 1840s even the extremely efficient and rapid coach service between London and Brighton had completely collapsed.

Many of the deeply conservative and snobbish patrons of select resorts and some of the tradesmen who catered for them, also viewed the coming of the railways with decided apprehension. There is a cartoon of the 1830s headed *Probable Effect of the Projected Rail-road to Brighton* which expresses this. It shows an elegant couple turning up their noses at a bow-legged, red-faced Cockney family who have arrived by train. 'Oh, we must leave this place,' says the gentleman, 'it may do for a Royal family, but not for a fashionable one.' 'What shocking savages!' agrees the lady.

The rapid working-class takeover of the seaside which the snobs had feared did not happen. The trains at first brought down to the coast far more of the same sort of prosperous, middle-class people who had been visiting the seaside since before the beginning of the nineteenth century; though all the changes produced by the Industrial Revolution meant that the number of people who now fell into this broad category had increased immensely. Fares were set low enough to ensure that coaches could offer no real

Cartoon for *Punch* by
John Leech, 1848

SEA-SIDE SATURDAY EVENING.—THE ARRIVAL OF THE "HUSBANDS' BOAT."

competition, but they were still well outside the reach of ordinary working people.

The first resorts which became truly popular and which long remained the favourites of people who cared nothing for gentility, were those that could be reached easily not by trains, but by steamboats. By the 1840s hundreds of steamers ferried passengers on pleasure trips from London past Gravesend to Margate (the water was too shallow at Southend for the steamers to land there), from Liverpool to the resorts at the mouth of the Mersey, the Isle of Man and North Wales, and from Scottish cities up the Firths of Forth and Clyde. Margate, the favourite of Londoners since the eighteenth century, was now unashamedly Cockney. 'Margate is what is termed vulgar,' said the *Illustrated Times* in 1856, 'that is to say it does not wear gloves, never dresses before dinner and likes rum and water with lemon in it.' The steamboats had taken over from the hoys in the 1820s and 'the fresh-painted Venus and iron-built Mars get up their steam, and side by side, pant and roar every morning at London Bridge whilst the mob of passengers fight and push across the gangways.'

There was a special Margate system of combining the family holiday with the demands of shop or office, and this was later adopted by other resorts. The wives and children of London tradesmen would stay in Margate all week and their husbands would join them at the weekend by 'the husbands' boat', an institution which was the subject of much jollity and innuendo, and of songs with titles like *What Ho She Bumps!* In the early 1860s the Great Vance had a hit in the halls with a song which gives a glimpse of the hearty atmosphere of the steamboats.

On Saturday according, the boat I soon was boarding
And with a lot of husbands got, a jolly set were we.
Imagine my surprise, when, I chanced to turn my eyes then
I saw a lovely damsel who was looking straight at me . . .

We got in conversation, I stood a cold collation;
We soon got near to Margate pier; the time went quickly by.
Around her taper waist, then, my arm I just had placed when
I heard a voice that brought me to my senses instantly . . .

My feelings won't bear painting, my wife with rage was
    fainting,
I'll draw a veil upon a scene so painfully severe.
    (Married Men!)
Be careful I entreat you; your wives may come to meet
    you;
Then take your arm away when you're in sight of Margate
    Pier.

THE EXCURSION TRAIN.

A TENDER . NARRATIVE :

SUNG BY
E. MARSHALL.
AT THE CANTERBURY HALL

WRITTEN EXPRESSLY FOR HIM BY   MUSIC ARRANGED BY
W. F. VANDERVELL . WILLEM VANDERVELL

Ent. Sta. Hall

Price 3/

LONDON
J. WILLIAMS 123 CHEAPSIDE

CONCANEN & LEE LITH.   STANNARD & DIXON, IMP.

The fares on the husband's boat were very low, 2s. or 1s. 6d. according to class in the mid-1850s, and even when railway excursions were at their cheapest, taking a steamboat to Margate was still usually the most economical way for Londoners to taste the pleasures of the seaside.

The invention of the excursion train, a typically Victorian combination of philanthropy and profit, marked the real beginning of the role of the railways in the recreation of the people as a whole. But it was only a beginning. The excursion trains allowed shop and factory workers to spend a carefree day or perhaps a weekend, by the sea, but it was not until the 1870s that many of them began to take longer holidays away from home. Before then, few working people could afford to take much unpaid time off work for a seaside jaunt, and holidays with pay were virtually unknown for manual workers before the 1880s.

Railway excursions to the seaside began in the 1840s. A whole train would be hired by a private firm or earmarked by the railway companies themselves and tickets sold at drastically reduced prices. For example, in 1844 a pioneering Lancashire manufacturer in benevolent mood took 650 of his employees on a pleasure trip to Fleetwood, and in the same year seven excursion trains, some of them consisting of thirty carriages, brought more than 2,000 passengers to Brighton on Easter Monday. *The Times* describes these excursionists as 'for the most part mechanics and their wives . . . dressed in their holiday attire'.

The great period for excursions was the 1850s. Innumerable cheap trips had been organized to bring visitors from all over the country to the Great Exhibition, and following their success the railway companies vied with each other to put on cheap excursions to the sea. Trips also began to be operated by professional travel agents with Thomas Cook in the lead and, especially in the north of England, all sorts of local bodies, Friendly Societies, Sunday Schools and Temperance Societies arranged them for their members. Employers began to feel that a visit to the seaside was a far less dangerous form of recreation for their work-people than the rough fairs and sports which had been their traditional way of spending their rare holidays. Fairs and football games almost always ended in drunken punch-ups, injuries and absenteeism. The seaside was comparatively respectable, innocent and healthy, and the sight of all that water was inspiring to the teetotal.

> Happy Cambourne, happy Cambourne,
> Where the seaside is so near,
> And the engine shows how water
> Can accomplish more than beer.

Opposite
Cover, by Concaven, for one of the many songs about the seaside that were popular from the mid-Victorian period, *c. 1870*

'To Brighton and Back for 3s. 6d.' became a popular catch-phrase – on a few trains in 1861 the fare was as low as 2s. 6d. – but excursion trains were still much slower than regular ones and they were often made up of uncomfortable open carriages. They were concentrated on traditional holidays like Easter and Whitsun and on Sundays, the only days on which most excursionists did not have to be at their shops or factories.

At Easter or Whitsun the resorts' ordinary middle-class patrons tended to melt away. They decided that it would be a good day to visit nearby ruins or go for a drive in the country; and on Sundays they were in church dressed in their best or parading about clutching 'the daintiest books of Common Prayer that money could buy', and the beach was left to the trippers. But because it was Sunday, which in the middle of the nineteenth century was kept with depressing strictness, a lot of the normal seaside amusements were denied the excursionists and in many resorts the entertainers and trinket-sellers were kept off the sands and the pleasure boats were beached for the day. (There was much pious agitation against the very act of travelling on Sundays – people like the Bishop of London spent long hours with the accident figures trying to prove God's wrath against Sabbath breakers, but this could not prevail against good sense, the National Sunday League and the powerful interests of the railway companies.)

The Sunday excursionists could still drink at the pubs and gin-shops in the back streets, eat their picnics and fool about on the sands. Here is a description of some of them in Brighton in 1862 from a book called *Brighton, the Road, the Place, the People.*

'They are not in the habit of resorting to the York or the Bedford, or even to hostelries of a humbler order. They bring their dinners with them in baskets, in sheets of old newspapers, and in pocket-handkerchiefs, and they dine in company at the "London Ordinary" a magnificent apartment under the cliff, having for its carpet the countless pebbles of the seashore, and for its roof the vaulted sky. The *carte* here is substantial, if not *recherché*. It comprises pork chops, cold; brisket of beef, ditto, cut with a hammy knife; bacon fried; knuckle of ham; and bread and cheese and onions. The liquors, chiefly ale and porter, are brought to the festive scene in stone bottles, which when emptied of their contents, being made cockshies of, turn up in sea-worn fragments after many years, to attract the eye of amateur collectors of curiosities, and find a place in some domestic museum of the treasures of the deep. The native inhabitants look down with supreme contempt upon these economical festivities; for all the delicacies of the season, even including the beer and the "drop of something short", are brought from London and Brighton reaps no benefit save from the extra pint that may be consumed as a supplementary treat in one of the numerous inferior houses of entertainment in which the town abounds.'

Brighton's contempt for the working-class excursionists was, in the mid-Victorian period, shared by most resorts which they visited. *Punch* reflected its genteel readers' attitudes, and almost every summer from the mid-fifties it has a prim piece on the vulgar seaside larks of 'Arry, 'Enry, 'Ugh and 'Umphrey. The 'trippers' – a word still pronounced with great disdain by elderly residents of south coast resorts – in spite of all the sneers, seem to have enjoyed themselves immensely at the seaside, but they had little influence on the character of most resorts until the last decades of the nineteenth century. Typical mid-Victorian seaside towns were still cosily middle-class and respectable, but their new railway stations opened the way for their later mass popularity.

Alice in Wonderland, with characteristic briskness, sums up the atmosphere of the seaside in the 1860s. 'Alice had been to the seaside once in her life, and had come to the general conclusion that, wherever you go on the English coast you find a number of bathing-machines in the sea, some children digging in the sand with wooden spades, than a row of lodging-houses, and behind them a railway station.'

Shells, Seaweed and Science

Shells, seaweed, pebbles and fossils fascinated the Victorians – collecting and classifying them and turning them into decorative and 'interesting' objects were minor mid-nineteenth-century obsessions, and an essential part of the middle-class family holiday.

The fashion for collecting shells had begun in England early in the eighteenth century. The poets, duchesses and aesthetes who started the craze were less interested in the modest English shells they could find at Weymouth or Scarborough than in exotic foreign rarities. They bought them expensively at auctions and bribed ships' captains to bring them back from the East and West Indies. Most of the great collectors of porcelain were also connoisseurs of shells; to them an especially beautiful or unusual shell, like

Cartoon for *Punch* by
John Leech, 1858

COMMON OBJECTS AT THE SEA-SIDE—GENERALLY FOUND UPON THE ROCKS AT LOW WATER.

those collected by Captain Cook, seemed as desirable as the most ancient and exquisite oriental vase. The Duchess of Portland spent a fortune on her great collection which filled scores of gilded cabinets in her private museum.

Eighteenth-century ladies were instructed by people like Mary Delany, a friend of the Duchess of Portland, on how to make complicated, delicate designs out of shells. She was a purist who disapproved of pictorial representation and insisted that shells should always be mounted on velvet and never tampered with or painted; and at this time amateur shell-craft was usually a hobby only for the dedicated. Shell ornaments made by professionals in the eighteenth century were also generally expensive and sophisticated rather than aimed at popular taste.

On the Continent follies and grottoes decorated with shells had been fashionable since the Renaissance, and early in the eighteenth century the idea was taken up by the English aristocracy. In 1739 the Duchess of Richmond and her daughters started decorating an enchanting little pavilion at Goodwood Park in Sussex. It took them seven years to cover the interior with white, pink and blue shells arranged in delicate classical patterns. Towards the end of the century an effect of Romantic gloom was more often aimed at. Landowners of sensibility had quantities of shells used to line caves for their hermits – they seemed to bring with them an echo of the sublime grandeur which was by then being attributed to the sea. Shell-lined grottoes became aristocratic status symbols. The Duke of York chose his, at Oaklands, to be the setting for the splendid banquet he held for the Tsar of Russia and other leaders of the victorious armies which had defeated Napoleon. Its walls shone in the candlelight with thousands of cowries and glistening white spar, and one of the corridors leading to the main chamber had been lined, to add a note of topicality, with the teeth of horses killed on the field of Waterloo.

It is strange that so few of these grottoes were made at the seaside, though some caves at Margate were known as 'the grotto', and there was a famous one built under the cliffs at Sidmouth, the most picturesque of the early resorts. It has now completely vanished, but in its day it was greatly admired. Through apertures in its walls could be seen views, 'such as would be experienced by Neptune surveying his kingdom from his rock castle in the ocean depths'. The whole interior was contrived of natural rock, open in places to the sky and festooned with shells, seaweed, fossils and moss. Visitors could sit on damp little iron chairs to admire the effect, or watch the birds of paradise in cages balanced on the rock ledges.

Most of the shells gathered in the long summer afternoons

by Georgian visitors to the seaside were probably not made into anything, or carefully arranged in cabinets, but admired for an evening, and then left behind forgotten in lodging-houses and attics – 'the pursuit of picking up shells is something to help the existence between breakfast and dinner.'

An increase in popular interest in shells coincided with the rise of the seaside resorts; gradually the fashion spread, and by the end of the eighteenth century marine libraries and seaside shops were selling choice specimens, and all sorts of natural objects of the seashore began to be prized as souvenirs. 'The variety of sea-weed, coralleries, pebbles and petrifactions to be met with on the rocks is very considerable,' writes a guide to Scarborough in 1813, 'but persons who prefer a less fatiguing mode of collecting may purchase very good specimens in the shops of the town.' By the 1840s many seaside resorts had a shop that specialized in selling shells. At Scarborough Mr Bean's provided Dr Granville with an intellectual treat, and at Poole in Dorset a lady called Polly Perkins became rich from turning local shells into necklaces and knick-knacks. She was famous for 'shell improving', varnishing, colouring, and touching-up specimens to suit the taste of visitors. Among the pedlars who thronged every Victorian beach there was always sure to be one selling trinkets made of shells, like the cockney dandy who irritated the crowds at Margate with his cry, 'A beautiful camellia after life in barnacle shells. Guaranteed all shells or I'll eat 'em.'

The soft luminous glow of shells exactly suited mass mid-Victorian taste; mother-of-pearl turned up everywhere at the time of the Great Exhibition, innumerable huge nautilus shells were imported and engraved with verses and pictures, sailors brought home big, octagonal shell Valentines from the West Indies and factories were set up in London where shell flower baskets were made on the assembly line principle – shaped like blancmanges and with bright, matte paint concealing all natural colour, these are often peculiarly hideous.

The seaside was always the best market for objects made of shells. A firm called Mr Samuel specialized in making cheap cardboard trinkets decorated with them for sale to the growing number of holidaymakers who did not have much money to spend on souvenirs, and pictures of resorts under domed glass framed in shells became popular in the second half of the century. Making shell-decorated boxes and needle-cases became a winter cottage-industry at many seaside resorts. At Margate shell animals were a local speciality. 'We had the opportunity of inspecting some very wonderful specimens of shell-work, really very ingenious

and perfect, in which by making the body of an animal or
bird with a speckled shell and adding legs, necks and tails of
a curious composition (a secret) like hard-baked pie crust,
a perfect resemblance to any living creature from a lion to
a cock is ensured. These images form excessively neat
chimney ornaments and by putting your ear to the animal's
stomach, you can hear by the noise of it's inside whether the
sea is rough or not.' (*Illustrated Times, 1856*)

Young ladies on holiday now collected shells with a new
energy and purpose. Back home, with the help of their
periodicals, they turned them into picture-frames and
boxes, decorated dolls' houses and looking glasses with them
and used scallops to edge the flower beds. Victorian girls
had a passion for making mosaics out of natural objects, it

Mid-Victorian souvenir
shell boxes

Overpage
Pegwell Bay Kent – a
Recollection of October
5th, 1858 by William Dyce

took up a lot of their endless spare time and was more fun than reading or doing Berlin woolwork. Seaweed was extremely popular for making pictures. The most common version was a basket of seaweed flowers nearly always inscribed with a verse which began—

> Oh, call us not weeds, but flowers of the sea,
> For lovely and gay and bright-tinted are we,
> Our blush is as deep as the rose in thy bowers,
> Then call us not weeds – we are oceans gay flowers.

It could also be twisted into the shapes of trees and even farm gates. Messrs Ackermann in the Strand provided patterns for 'very beautiful seaweed landscapes'.

Highly polished pebbles were also considered ornamental, and a good lapidary could make £100 or £150 a year from polishing pebbles 'without doing any night work in a good watering-place in the south of England'. Some resorts had their own particular specialities. On the Isle of Wight in the 1840s a group of craftsmen, making pictures and glass paperweights out of the brightly coloured variegated sands of Alum Bay, was established at Newport. The best-known of them was called Edwin Dore, and his little sand pictures of Shanklin Chine or Carisbrooke Castle were eagerly bought by visitors to the island.

At Whitby in Yorkshire, and in Scarborough, all sorts of jewellery, miniature furniture and ornaments were made out of jet. When Dr Granville was in Scarborough in the 1840s highly finished jet 'necklaces, chains of every variety of pattern, crosses, waist-buckles, paper-folders and rings' could be bought for 'about one-fourth of what would be asked for them in London'.

Cornish serpentine rock, mottled and richly coloured, was carved into vases and boxes, or models of Cleopatra's Needle or the Eddystone Lighthouse for sale in the West Country, and semi-precious stones found on the sea-shore, like amber and cornelian, began to be admired and made into all sorts of jewellery.

But by the mid-nineteenth century the 'treasures of the shore' were being sought after for more than their decorative possibilities. By the 1850s and 1860s there was much public excitement about the developments that were being made in the natural sciences. This was partly because some of the new scientific theories did not coincide with accepted religious beliefs. Geological researches at the beginning of the century had begun the questioning of orthodox Old Testament doctrines about the sudden creation of the world, and with the publication of Darwin's *Origin of Species*

Opposite
Mid-Victorian doll, dressed as a shell-fish pedlar – probably the work of an amateur shell enthusiast

in 1859 the controversy became intense. But these conflicts between science and religion do not seem to have made the study of natural history any less respectable, they simply made it more exciting and important. 'The humble and faithful study of nature' was advocated by Ruskin, and all sorts of eminent and literary Victorians, like George Eliot, took to poring intensely over rock pools or chasing butterflies or classifying pebbles. These amateur naturalists took themselves very seriously, they gave their hobbies impressive scientific names, and felt that their patient detailed studies were morally uplifting. As Charles Kingsley wrote in *Glaucus or the Wonders of the Shore*, 'The qualifications required for a perfect naturalist are as many and as lofty as were required by the old chivalrous writers for the perfect knight errant of the middle ages.'

The seashore was the favourite of all hunting-grounds, partly because, while most land plants and animals had already been classified, it was still possible for the amateur to discover new species there and, as Kingsley said, add 'his mite to the treasures of science', and partly because at the seaside there was even more time than usual to be filled improvingly.

Marine life was the subject of particularly able popularizers. One of the most interesting and influential of them was Philip Gosse, a tragic figure torn between professional objectivity and a rigid religious fundamentalism. For many years he studied the shore life of Devon and Cornwall. He spent his days, accompanied by his small son Edmund, wading shoulder-high in search of rare specimens, and his evenings observing, classifying and painting them with minute attention to detail. Edmund, whose eyesight was particularly sharp, would stay for hours bent over the tanks; looking, he says, as if he were about to wash his hair among the anemones and describing to his father every activity of the tiny sea creatures.

Philip Gosse's series of books began with *A Naturalist's Rambles on the Devonshire Coast* published in 1854 and included *The Aquarium* and *A Year at the Shore*. Both he and his friend Kingsley held summer seaside classes in marine biology and he started a fashion for domestic aquariums. (Ways of keeping sea creatures alive in captivity had only recently been discovered. Gosse's own collection had formed the nucleus of the first marine aquarium to be set up in England by the Royal Zoological Society in Regent's Park in 1852.) Gosse instructed his readers on suitable specimens, the correct fixing of rocks, and the right balance of plants and animals. It was a fairly laborious process. Sea-water was to be obtained by 'giving a trifling fee to the master or steward of any of the steamers that ply beyond the mouth

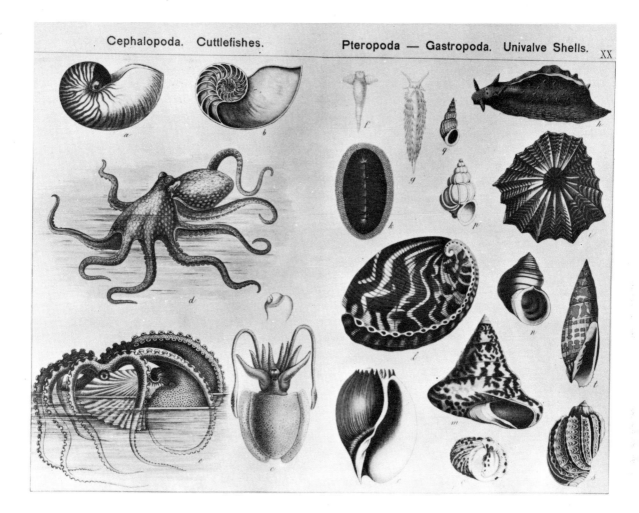

of the Thames, and charging him to dip a flask into the clear open sea, beyond the reach of rivers'. Fishes and plants should be sent by mail-train and forwarded immediately by special messenger. Soon, as with shell collecting, shop-keepers came to the aid of amateur enthusiasts. At Mr Lloyd's shop in Portland Place which stocked more than 15,000 specimens, sea cucumbers and anemones could be bought at prices ranging from sixpence to seven shillings.

In 1862 Mrs Gatty, a well-known writer of stories for children and evangelical works, published her book *British Seaweeds*. It was an instant best-seller. The book was written specifically for her own sex and it must have been marvellously liberating reading for every suppressed Victorian tomboy. In the days when croquet was the only respectable sport for ladies, she encouraged them to scramble over the roughest rocks wearing 'boy's shooting boots made water-proof by a coating of neat's foot oil as used by fishermen'. The wet would be too much for even 'the best pair of single-

A plate from *The Natural History of the Animal Kingdom for the Use of Young People*. Published by The Society for Promoting Christian Knowledge

97

TERRIFIC ACCIDENT.

BURSTING OF OLD MRS. TWADDLE'S AQUA-VIVARIUM. THE OLD LADY MAY BE OBSERVED ENDEAVOURING TO PICK UP HER FAVOURITE EEL WITH THE TONGS, A WORK REQUIRING SOME ADDRESS.

Cartoon for *Punch* by John Leech, *c.* 1860

soled Balmoral boots'. She didn't go as far as her much-ridiculed contemporary, Amelia Bloomer, and suggest the discarding of petticoats, 'though if anything could excuse a woman from imitating the costume of a man, it would be what she suffers as a seaweed collector from those necessary draperies'. In yachting costumes of practical blue serge, carrying baskets lined with gutta-percha and having seen to it that luncheon coincided with high tide, her girls were ready for the attack; but even the dashing Mrs Gatty recommended a male companion for the most 'eerie' and dangerous rocks. 'He may fossilize, or sketch, or even, if he will be savage and barbaric, shoot gulls (though one had rather not); but no need anyhow to involve him in messing after what he may consider rubbish; unless happily he may be inclined to assist.'

Seaweed hunters' evenings were spent crawling about on hotel floors, cleaning their evil-smelling specimens in bowls of salt and fresh water, laying them out with porcupine quills, and checking their scientific nomenclature against

Mrs Gatty's eighty coloured plates. She continued to collect seaweed for the rest of her life and sold her albums of specimens for large sums to support charitable causes. Queen Victoria requested one of them, perhaps it brought back memories, for she herself had been a pioneer seaweed collector as a child, and it gave the final seal of respectability to a messy and exhilarating hobby.

By the 1880s the craze was waning. Domestic marine aquariums were being abandoned, as it had proved extremely difficult to keep the animals alive. Collecting was either left to professionals or, like other short-lived seaside amusements, donkey-riding for instance, taken over by children. Kingsley's *The Water Babies* introduced the undersea world to the imaginations of generations of children, and by the end of the century the rock pools had become their province.

In *Father and Son* published in 1907, Edmund Gosse has a sad postscript. 'The ring of living beauty drawn about our shores was a very thin and fragile one. It existed all these centuries solely in consequence of the indifference, the blissful ignorance of man. These rock basins fringed with corallines, filled with still water, almost as pellucid as the upper air itself, thronged with beautiful, sensitive forms of life – they exist no longer, they are profaned, and emptied and vulgarised. An army of collectors had passed over them and ravaged every corner of them. The fairy paradise has been violated, the exquisite product of centuries of natural selection has been crushed under the rough paw of well-meaning, idle minded curiosity. That my father, himself so reverent, so conservative, had by the popularity of his books acquired the direct responsibility for a calamity that he had never anticipated became clear enough to himself before many years had passed and caused him great chagrin. No-one will see again on the shores of England, what I saw in my early childhood, the submarine vision of dark rocks, speckled and starred with an infinite variety of colour, and streamed over by silken flags of royal crimson and purple.'

'You Can Do a Lot of Things at the Seaside...'

> By the sea! By the sea!
> The beautiful silvery sea!
> Where you hear the brass band play
> 'Yip-I-addy-I-ay'
>
> With your girlie, girlie,
> That's where you want to be,
> Down on the sands, on the silvery sands,
> By the side of the silvery sea.

sang Mark Sheridan, strutting about in his battered top-hat and bell-bottomed trousers. By the turn of the century there were hundreds of popular songs about the seaside. 'You can do a lot of things at the seaside that you can't do in town,' went another.

> Fancy seeing mother with her legs all bare,
> Paddling in the fountains of Trafalgar Square.

In smoky, beery, music-halls all over England the audiences were joining in the choruses with feeling. They *did* like to be beside the sea. The seaside, like the music-hall itself, had become a great popular entertainment, a relief from the drudgery and restraints of everyday life – a huge joke that, it seemed then, could never go stale.

In England in the period between 1880 and 1914 many medium-sized resorts were at the height of their prosperity and popularity. Families would affectionately adopt a particular resort and return there year after year – it became an important part of their lives, a second, but far more exciting, home town. Mr Pooter, the archetypal late-nineteenth-century little man, and the hero of *The Diary of A Nobody*, always relished the thought of his annual week's holiday at 'Good Old Broadstairs'.

The Ancient Wrasse, a colour plate by Philip Gosse from *A Year at the Shore*, 1856

A seaweed picture by E. Griesbach, mid-nineteenth century

'Spooning' on the sands at
Yarmouth in the 1890s
Photograph by Paul
Martin

It was now quite usual for clerks like Mr Pooter, shop assistants, and some factory workers – the kind of people who made up most music-hall audiences – to get a week's holiday with pay. There were now more clubs and organizations that encouraged saving, and cheaper, better third-class travel. Day trips were as popular as ever, especially on Bank Holidays, which had been introduced in 1871, and some working-class people in England could at last afford to stay at a resort for a week or so. They came determined to enjoy their temporary freedom, and they brought with them a new boisterous exuberance. 'Awfully naughty place,' wrote Richard Jefferies of Brighton beach in high summer in the 1880s, 'no sort of idea of rightness here. Humming and strumming and singing and smoking, splashing and sparkling, a buzz of voices and a booming of sea! If only they could be happy like this always.'

There were still, of course, many millions of people in England who could not afford to take even a day's holiday away from home; and many city children who had never seen the sea. There is a Du Maurier cartoon in *Punch* of 1886 headed 'These Yellow Sands' which shows a scene that must have been repeated hundreds of times every summer. A group of pinched, shabby children are shown staring with 'wistful admiration' at the Brown family setting off laden with buckets and spades and tennis rackets for the station and the seaside.

This longing was exploited by advertisers. All sorts of dubious money-making schemes were presented as methods of saving for a seaside holiday. 'The Annual Seaside Holiday How Is It Done?' asks a poster of the 1880s with a picture of two moustachioed swells raising their hats to some elegant ladies on the beach. 'Why, by saving, all the Year Round, your Old Clothes, Bones, Rags, Waste Paper, and in fact Lumber of any kind, and bringing them to this Shop where you will get Good Prices, Fair Dealing and Civility.' The seaside had become the dream setting for a good time, something to save up and work for.

The middle classes, people like Du Maurier's Browns, confidently mingled on the beaches and the promenade with people who at home would have been making their hats or serving them with groceries, but at night they retreated to 'superior' accommodation. When they became particularly fastidious about the company, they could always move to a quiet, as yet 'undiscovered' resort. The pattern established at the end of the eighteenth century, by which some resorts were considered far more respectable and genteel than others, was continued and elaborated. 'The "anti-tripper",' wrote Bernard Becker, in his *Holiday Haunts* of 1880, 'has left the breezy coasts and superb sands of the popular bathing towns and sought out-of-the-way villages . . . in which ears polite are not vexed with barrel-organs and music-hall choruses. Hence a vast number of new watering-places have been developed. . . . As they become popular, the ingenious anti-tripper moves on and opens up a new Filey for every Scarborough, a new Lowestoft for every Yarmouth.' Frinton, the most self-consciously respectable resort in England, was founded soon after the turn of the century. Even today, it does not have a pub, let alone a pier.

Most old-established English resorts are still full of the buildings, objects and atmosphere of their late Victorian and Edwardian prime; and perhaps the most potent of all the seaside memorials to this vanished golden age are the piers that stick out like exclamation marks all round the English coast. By the 1880s piers had become the great seaside

Paddlers, 1890s
Photograph by Paul
Martin

status symbols. Resorts rivalled each other in the length, elaboration and – if they were extremely prosperous – number of their piers. The eighties was the decade when the greatest number of English piers were built, and when resorts which had already acquired them were adding imposing new buildings to their decks. The opening of a pier was often seen as the beginning of a glorious new lease of life for a resort, and as a gesture of welcome to 'the many'; an acknowledge- ment that most resorts could no longer afford to depend entirely on people who could provide their own amusement who 'came with their horses and carriages . . . staying five or six weeks'. Everyone found the new piers exciting. Quick profits were made by the companies that financed them and they were 'resorted to freely by all classes'.

They are still extraordinary structures – perhaps the most

The Chain Pier, Brighton.
Photographed from its
head, *c.* 1870

impressive surviving examples of Victorian popular design, and certainly the best people's fun palaces yet invented.

Their history really began with the Chain Pier at Brighton, the grandest and most famous pier of the first half of the nineteenth century.

> But of all the sweet pleasures that
>   Brighton can boast,
> A walk on the Chain Pier delighted me most,
> That elegant structure, light, airy and free,
> Like a work of enchantment hangs over the sea.

went a verse of the song written specially for its opening in 1823, which still conjures up some of the special charm of pier-walking.

Margate was probably the first seaside town where visitors made a habit of going for strolls on the stone boat jetty to enjoy the sea air. Pedlars and entertainers set up booths there, a band sometimes played and a penny entrance was charged. The Chain Pier, however, was built not only as a landing-stage for the ships setting off for Dieppe, but also specifically for fashionable promenading. The prospectus claimed that the pier company would make a profit of at least £10 a day by charging people just to walk about on it, and it was designed with room for little shops and stalls at the foot of its four tapering towers. They were let to people who sold refreshments and souvenirs, china 'inscribed with Christian names, or with "A Present from Brighton", together with shells and toys in spun glass', there were

Eastbourne Pier, *c.* 1900

lots of telescopes, a specialist in wax flowers and a silhouette artist. J. Gapp would cut a likeness for 2*s.* 6*d.*, and his successor advertised, as a sideline, 'a weighing-machine and two very superior new pleasure boats'. The resident Brighton fireworks expert let off rockets into the night from a platform at the end of the pier, where on fine mornings a band played and the packet-boat embarked.

From the time it first opened the Chain Pier was a great popular success, despite complaints about the entrance fee. 'Here for the sum of twopence,' wrote Thackeray, 'you can go out to sea and pace this vast deck without need of a basin.' William IV loved to stride about on it distributing sweets to children and imagining himself far out to sea. His subjects followed his example, and the pier was crowded with bath-chairs and elegant promenaders. But by the 1870s the crowds had deserted the Chain Pier. It had been eclipsed by the new West Pier which opened in 1866. Having fallen into disrepair, the old Chain Pier cheated the demolition men by being finally swept away in the great storm of 1896.

Although in its atmosphere and amusements the Chain Pier was the direct ancestor of the later piers, structurally it was quite different from its successors. It was designed by a naval architect, Captain Samuel Brown, and was, in effect, one of the first of the great suspension bridges of the nineteenth century. The later piers followed the same basic pattern as the West Pier at Brighton, which was supported on a lattice of thin iron columns. Their decks often bulged out at the end, where the buildings were concentrated – 'from the stem, like a fair flower, the head expands', as the brochure for the opening of Cromer Pier put it.

Most of the civil engineers who built the late Victorian piers were more concerned with the complex problems of making them longer and wider and completely storm-proof than with their appearance. Yet they were often marvellously decorative. The pavilions, restaurants, shelters and theatres on the pier decks generally had their iron frames bolted to the heads of the supporting columns sunk into the sea-bed, so that they looked as if they were growing satisfyingly straight up out of the water. The manner in which they were constructed contributes to the feeling of lightness and unity characteristic of the best English piers, and so does the exuberant, vaguely oriental style which seemed a natural choice for pier buildings.

This oriental influence was part of a tradition that went back to the eighteenth century. Chinese, Moorish and Hindu-inspired forms had long been associated with buildings made purely for pleasure. Eighteenth-century nobles decorated their parks with pagodas and little Hindu temples, and the Brighton Pavilion was the culmination of this aristocratic fashion. Though very few houses were influenced by its design, similar tent-like shapes, onion domes and filigree ironwork were used later in public pleasure gardens like Vauxhall and Cremorne. The Chinese dancing pavilion at Cremorne was an elaborate iron pagoda, and the Eagle Tavern in the City Road, one of the most popular Victorian pleasure gardens, had a skyline of pointed domes and minarets.

In the 1860s and 1870s when the earliest iron piers were being built, the London pleasure gardens were rapidly declining. The piers took over not only many of their amusements – fireworks, dancing, music, sideshows, lights – but also their characteristic oriental shapes.

'A fine pavilion occupies the centre, and viewed from the exterior reminds one of some eastern palace,' says a Blackpool guide of the 1890s about the Victoria Pier; and though many piers are now marred by crude later additions, some still have this feeling about them. From a distance, the piers at Eastbourne and Southsea, for instance, have the look of stately oriental pleasure-domes suspended over the sea; and in Brighton where the influence of the Pavilion must have been most direct, the Palace Pier, the prettiest in England, is still covered with silvery minarets and onion domes.

Pier amusements have not changed much, but at the turn of the century they were perhaps more varied than they are today. They usually included performing fleas, fortune-tellers, terrifying diving displays – 'professors' would plunge into the sea, handcuffed or enveloped in flames – cameras obscura for looking at enchanting miniature reflections of the town, trick cyclists and roller-skating rinks. There were always the crowds of silent men fishing hopefully from the lower decks, and local entertainment committees soon began to organize competitions and sea-angling festivals. You could dance, too, or drink tea, or listen to the band. And when you had had enough you could catch one of the big new paddle-steamers and go for a thrilling voyage, chugging down the coast.

The slot-machines which are now so much a part of the rather raffish atmosphere of piers began to appear in about 1900. Brighton and Blackpool specialized in handmade clockwork models of gruesome scenes that jerked into life for a penny. 'The Guillotine', 'The Haunted House', and 'The Execution of Mary Queen of Scots' were great favourites, and there were mechanical fortune-tellers, less embarrassing and expensive than the real thing, machines that administered health-giving electric shocks, and coy 'What the Butler Saw' machines.

Piers had a very liberating effect on people. 'There are young ladies, perfectly decorous and well-behaved in London,' wrote a shocked contributor to *The Queen* in 1900, 'who give themselves up to a general *abandon* on piers which is astonishing.'

The seaside pier is characteristically but not exclusively English: there are similar, though less decorative piers at some Dutch and Belgian resorts; and there are scores, perhaps hundreds, of them in the United States. No English resort has ever boasted as many piers as Atlantic City which in the 1930s had six, including 'Young's Million Dollar Pier'. Atlantic City, with its suitably named suburbs of Ventnor and Margate, was at the end of the nineteenth century more like a popular English resort than any other American seaside town. Its first pier, an imitation of those going up in England, was built in 1881, and was one of the earliest in the States. Most American and continental piers were constructed on the same basic principle as the English ones and offered much the

same kind of amusement, but their decks are often completely covered with buildings which have none of the oriental feeling of their English counterparts, and they tend to look top-heavy and lumpish instead of graceful.

At the beginning of this century some of the growing American resorts, like Venice in California, began to erect thrilling alternatives to piers, enormous roller-coasters built out over the sea. They must have been tremendously exciting to ride on, but perhaps the thrills were rather too real, for they became notorious for accidents. The big dipper on Clacton Pier, one of the first in England, was not put up till the 1930s and is tame compared with the much earlier American giants.

There was one extremely imaginative American experiment with piers that is worth recording, although it is not strictly concerned with the seaside. In the 1890s the sociologist Jacob A. Riis organized the building of several piers projecting out into the East River in New York near some of the city's worst slums: 'great, handsome structures, seven hundred feet long some of them. . . . The street is far away with its noise.' They were called 'Play Piers' and were

Pier at Atlantic City, a double-decker, quite different in style from English piers. Photograph by Muybridge, 1892

109

Roller-coaster at Venice,
California, *c.* 1900

financed chiefly by the City of New York, no entrance money
was charged. In the day time free nursery schools for slum
children were organized on the decks away from the stifling
heat of the city, and in the evening the piers were
crowded with people escaping from their tenements to enjoy
the breezes from the river, the bands and the moonlight.

In many of the English resorts, by the 1880s, the intricate
ironwork of the piers was continued all along the seafronts.
The promenades were edged with curly iron railings and
punctuated by tall lamp-posts wreathed in coloured lights,
odd little iron-framed shelters, and magnificent bandstands. The stirring music of the bands had become an
essential part of the gaiety of a stroll along the esplanade,
and late Victorian seaside bandstands are often particularly
fine specimens. At Scarborough they were elaborate rotundas
at each end of the promenade – when both bands were
playing at once, a walk was particularly bracing. The
'Birdcage Bandstand' on the front at Brighton, with its
shallow dome and delicate cast iron tracery is typical in
shape and spirit of many others dotted around the coast.
The shelters built overlooking the sea often repeated the
shapes of the shelters on the piers. Like the railings along the

promenades, much of the pier detailing, and sometimes even the bandstands, they were in general not specifically designed for their seaside sites, but were bought off the peg, chosen by the local borough surveyor from the catalogues of the great foundries which produced huge ranges of designs in cast iron. Much of the Victorian ironwork for the Sussex resorts was designed and made at an iron foundry in Lewes – the same one that half a century earlier had produced the cast iron for the beautiful balconies and railings of Regency Brighton – but most other seaside towns bought their cast iron from the big foundries in the midlands and the north.

There was a new feeling of spaciousness about prosperous late Victorian resorts. The promenades were continually being widened, often with walks at several different levels. Sometimes, as at Eastbourne, wide strips of lawn ran the whole length of the parade. They were set with bulging beds of contrasting flowers or the town crest carefully picked out in geraniums and lobelias. Cliff walks were turned into romantic gardens, like Shanklin Chine on the Isle of Wight. Big new parks were laid out – at Bournemouth the whole town was opened up by a central garden with winding paths and monkey-puzzles. New wide straight roads were cut at right angles to the seafront – according to Victorian planners they made a resort more imposing, and they provided with their distant views of the sea continual reminders of the reason for the town's existence. At Hove and Eastbourne half the streets end in a framed line of sea and an expanse of sky.

As they increased in size, resorts began to experiment with all sorts of new ways of transporting people about – not just to get them from the pier to a hotel half a mile away along the promenade, but as irresistible mechanical toys for joy-riding. Hydraulic railways were built at many places, Hastings and Bournemouth for instance, to make cliff-top walks less strenuous; new tram-cars took crowds to the end of the long piers at Southport and Southend, and miniature railways, the delight of little boys, began to puff along beside the waves. The craziest and most original of all was Magnus Volk's 'Daddy-long-legs' at Brighton. In 1883 Volk's Electric Railway running along the seafront became one of the most popular attractions of the town. It was an impressive novelty, the first electric railway to provide a public service in the whole of Britain, and its little canopied cars sliding along at six miles an hour were packed. Volk gradually extended his line, and because it was impossible to take it over the cliffs to Rottingdean, he had the brilliant inspiration of laying the track along the beach, where it would be covered by the sea at high tide, and

Shanklin Chine, Isle of Wight, a romantic cliff walk. From *The Album of Isle of Wight Views*

Volk's Railway Poster, *c.* 1896

mounting the carriages on tall, spindly iron legs. They looked like Pullman cars on stilts gliding miraculously above the water, or bits of the pier that were slowly escaping.

The Daddy-long-legs was short-lived – it only ran from 1896 to 1900 – but had its great moment when the Prince of Wales went for a ride on it in 1897 and it was a perfect seaside combination of functionalism and unselfconscious fantasy.

Towards the end of the nineteenth century the bigger seaside towns were establishing themselves as the best provincial centres in the country for every kind of entertainment. This is particularly true of some which were far from all the attractions of London. Bernard Becker says in his chapter on the pleasures of Scarborough in *Holiday Haunts*: 'Existence in a weaving or spinning town is very different from what is called life in London . . . in a large number of wealthy industrial towns in the north of England the population is hungry and thirsty for amusement.' They got it lavishly and variously in Scarborough – 'The Spa Theatre and Londesborough Theatre are in full blast, Mr. Kelly has just done the first, and Miss Ada Cavendish is playing at the second. Mr. Sims Reeves is to sing and there are to be balls at various hotels on various pretexts' – and at many other resorts, at Bournemouth, or nearer London, at Eastbourne. Blackpool, which deserves a chapter almost to itself, was marvellously successful in this respect. Seaside municipal orchestras were founded, the stars of the music-hall and opera gave recitals, new theatres were built, race meetings were held and, as sport had recently become the fashion, tennis courts, cricket grounds and golf courses were laid out.

Cricket weeks and tennis tournaments were organized as part of the attractions of the summer season. When there were no county matches being played at Hastings, the Wanderers took on the Gasworks, or the local butchers played the butchers of Eastbourne. Lawn-tennis became one of the smartest pastimes at resorts frequented by the upper-middle classes. Du Maurier young men and girls became seaside 'lawntennysonians', and it was chic to stroll about the town all day in white tennis flannels with a little cap pulled down over one eye and a racket always in one's hand, 'like the riding whip and spurs affected by a bygone generation'.

To house some of the new entertainments, a new kind of characteristic seaside building began to be constructed in the 1870s and 1880s. These were the winter gardens, seaside Crystal Palaces, which could be used for dances and concerts. They were also, as their name implies, out-of-season meeting places for the growing number of permanent

The Floral Hall on the Parade at Bridlington, *c.* 1910

residents who were building themselves detached villas on the outskirts of coastal towns; and like the shelters on the prom, they were also an acknowledgement of the fact that, even in summer, it often rained. Usually the winter gardens were big, iron-framed, barn-like structures, filled with palm trees, banks of flowers and little tables for taking tea, while a string trio in the background swooped through selections from the popular classics. They made genteel retreats from the brashness and brass bands outside.

A few of the most prosperous resorts also built public aquariums, for though the craze for trying to keep sea-creatures alive in tanks in the drawing-room had died down, there was still a great deal of fashionable interest in them. Gothic was considered the most suitable style. They were romantic and instructive places – dim, underground cathedrals with peering octupuses and electric eels instead of stained glass windows, and they were somewhere else to go when it was wet.

The Brighton Aquarium was opened in 1872. It was designed by Eusebius Birch, the engineer and designer of the West Pier, who was also responsible for a similarly Gothic but less successful aquarium at Scarborough. At once, the new Brighton establishment became extremely smart. 'Unquestionably the most popular resort in the town,' says a guide of the 1880s. 'It is probably the grandest aquarium in the world and not only gives unequalled facilities for insight into life beneath the waters, but furnishes an agreeable lounge and place of amusement where visitors may congregate irrespective of the weather.' As well as the fishes there were organ recitals in the entrance hall, displays by Japanese court jugglers, 'Madame Emmeline Nicolo in her drawing-room entertainment of Magic and Mystery, Introducing her Inimitable Vanishing Lady Trick', and 'Merrie Little Rosie the Child Transformation Queen'.

Down on the beaches, in spite of all grand new amusements, there were still the crowds of pedlars, 'professors', and Punch and Judy men, and now the Salvation Army often played and sang and all sorts of other evangelists 'strove to sow good seeds among the holiday-makers'. In 1896 a new kind of entertainment made its debut on the sands. Will Catlin's Pierrots playing on the beach at Scarborough were so successful that soon the pale wistful pierrot had completely eclipsed the hearty black-faced nigger minstrel and become the most popular of all seaside entertainers.

The pierrots, whose ancestry goes back to the Commedia dell'Arte and the Funambules in Paris, had first appeared in their debased, but charming, English form in 1891, when a group of well-known singers had the idea of disguising themselves in ruffles, pompoms and skullcaps to serenade the crowds at Henley Regatta from a punt on the river. Unlike the minstrel bands, these troupes often included girls, who made very pretty pierrettes. They would all stand around a piano or harmonium – on the sands if it was fine or 'if wet under the pier' – and do little comic sketches and sing rather melancholy songs which seem often to have been about the moon. At the end of the show, before the audience had had time to leave their deckchairs, they would take a collection – 'bottling' was the term used in the profession – saying with a gentlemanly smile, 'Patronize the Pierrots'.

The pierrot troupes were given names like the Cigarettes, the White Coons, Arcady, the Beaux and Belles or the Biscuits, names which conjure up the touch of class and the nonchalant romance that they brought to the seaside. By

116

1914 they and the rival concert parties, the fol-de-rols and the follies, who did much the same kind of show without the help of such endearing costumes, were often performing in comfort on stages at the end of the pier. As the sun went down and the stars came out and the coloured gas lamps were lit on the parade, their tinkling songs could be heard from far away drifting out over the empty beaches.

By the mid-nineteenth century it was quite common for middle-class men to be able to swim; and by the end of the century it was expected of them. It was by then a sport taught in many public schools and subjected to rules and regulations by the Amateur Swimming Association which had been set up in 1886. In 1875 the Channel had been swum from Dover to Calais for the first time by Captain Webb. His success was the talk of England and inspired many young men to perfect their breast-stroke.

And swimming was becoming an acceptable activity even for women. 'We hope our fair readers will not be shocked if we say a few words about swimming, which is considered by some to be an unfeminine accomplishment,' began the author of an article in a ladies' magazine in the 1860s. 'The chief drawback to ladies swimming', she went on, 'is the bathing dress used in this country.' But by the 1880s

Bathing dresses hanging up to dry, 1909

women were no longer wearing long, flapping woolly gowns, but comparatively functional costumes with a skirt to somewhere above the knee, over 'full drawers' to somewhere below it. They were made of materials with names like Devonshire Serge or Turkey Twill and ornamented with 'bands, rays and a fringed sash in ecru' or puffed sleeves and sailor collars, and worn with 'thread stockings for decency's sake'. Gradually the stockings and the overskirts were discarded and they became one-piece costumes in which it was really possible to swim.

In the 1860s girls had felt daring when they bobbed up and down in the water with one foot off the bottom, but as sport became more fashionable and women took up cricket and golf, swimming classes for ladies were held on many beaches and others learnt to swim in the privacy of indoor baths, like the special ladies' pool which was an extension of Brill's Baths at Brighton. Some athletic girls even learnt to dive, and there is a report of one intrepid sixteen-year-old who for a bet swam a quarter of a mile fully clothed. She wore not only, 'all the ordinary under garments of a lady,

French bathing-beauty from *Les Saisons*, Paris 1900

including corsets, but also a heavy Fishwife-serge dress, boots, hat and gloves, carrying in one hand a huge scarlet Turkey twill umbrella opened, and in the other a large bouquet of somewhat gaudy flowers. . . . She, of course, could not use her arms at all, being obliged to hold them well out of the water for the preservation of the umbrella and bouquet, and therefore propelled herself entirely with her legs, arriving on shore safely, amidst the cheers of an admiring crowd.'

The new women's bathing-costumes were not only comparatively practical, they were attractive and, by the standards of the time, revealing. Seaside glamour was having a great revival, and in the years before the turn of the century the bathing-beauty was born. She seems to have been a continental invention; and although there has always been an element of fantasy about her, she was based on fact.

French women had long been famous for their fascinating appearance in the water. The trouble they took was perhaps influenced by the mixed bathing, but unlike Englishwomen, they had always refused to abandon elegance in the sea. They got their dressmakers to soak their bathing-costumes before they tried them on so that they could judge how they would look when they were wet, and they made a point of wearing corsets under them to retain their wasp-waists in the water. In the 1880s the commercial artists who specialized in sophisticated, titillating pictures for magazines like *La Vie Parisienne* began to realize the possibilities of bathing-costumes, and by the 1890s heavily touched up photographs of girls in impossibly low-cut costumes wading in the sea or lying in front of painted backdrops of breaking waves had become extremely popular. They were published in albums and, from about 1903, as postcards for sale all over Europe. Continental illustrators began to draw seaside sirens in bathing-costumes far more revealing and seductive than anything that can ever have been seen on the beaches, and some of their postcards were considered immoral by the English authorities and suppressed.

"I AM FEELING VERY LONELY!"
COME DOWN AND SPLASH ME.
AT YARMOUTH

The bathing-beauty soon captured the imagination of Edwardian Englishmen and Americans, and the image of beaches populated entirely with delicious sex symbols began to be one of the standard male fantasies—

> All the girls are lovely by the seaside,
> All the girls are lovely by the sea . . .

went a popular song.

Bathing-beauty contests did not take place until after the First World War, but long before then the seaside

French and English postcard bathing-beauties. The Yarmouth belle is an early Donald McGill

had begun to seem once again, as it had in the eighteenth century, the best place of all for girl-watching.

Bathing-machines were growing more and more unpopular. Every summer *Punch* attacked them with jokes, cartoons and rhymes. Here is one with the title *A Study of a Rare Old Conservative* that appeared in 1883.

It is not aesthetic, not yet picturesque,
'Tis heavy, and cumbrous, expensive, grotesque,
And I feel very certain there never was seen,
Such an old-fashioned thing as the Bathing Machine . . .
Oh, a hideous hutch is the Bathing Machine.

In the years before the First World War, at last bathing-machines began to be dispensed with. Sometimes they were permanently beached above the high-water mark and turned into changing-rooms, or they were replaced by white-painted wooden huts or tents.

In England bathing-machines and the separation of the sexes in the water went together; and this too began to seem increasingly ridiculous. Mixed bathing on the continental model became a favourite topic of conversation and was the subject of several music-hall songs. 'Should the sexes bathe together?' sang Marie Lloyd.

That is the question now
'Certainly! most decidedly!' Is the sort of
answer they get from me.

One of the first resorts in England to allow mixed bathing was Bexhill in Sussex where it was approved in 1901, but even by 1914 there were some old-fashioned seaside towns which still insisted on segregation.

Many people dispensed with all the bother and expense of buying bathing-costumes and hiring machines or huts by just paddling. For anyone over the age of ten it was considered tripperish and vulgar, but this did not worry the fathers who rolled up their trouser-legs and paddled about with their bowler hats on and their pipes in their mouths, or the mothers who safety-pinned their skirts, making sure they 'weren't showing too much bare leg' and cooled off their poor feet in the breakers.

The sea itself, 'the beautiful, silvery sea', could still be awe-inspiring. Edwardian holidaymakers often found it mysterious and frightening, but that only added to its fascination. The calmest trip around the bay seemed a thrilling adventure; and fishermen, whose trade it was to battle with storms and defy the elements, were at this

Opposite, above
Revere Beach, Maurice Prendergast, 1896

Opposite, below
Brighton Pierrots, W. R Sickert, 1915

121

This Song may be Sung in public without fee or licence, except at Theatres and Music Halls.

BATHING

Written by J. P. HARRINGTON,

Composed by GEORGE LE BRUNN.

CHORUS.
Where's the harm? where's the harm? will anyone tell me pray?
If the sexes bathe together,
In the beautiful summer weather,
When they tell you it's wrong, tell 'em to take a run,
Go along, do, with your old Mother Hubbard,
And don't come spoiling the fun!

WAITING FOR MARIE'S TURN.

Sung by
MISS MARIE LLOYD.

Copyright.

Price 4/-

LONDON: FRANCIS, DAY & HUNTER, 142 CHARING CROSS ROAD, (OXFORD STREET END,)
Publishers of, Smallwood's Celebrated Pianoforte Tutor. Smallwood's 55 Melodious Exercises, Etc.
NEW YORK: T. B. HARMS & Cº 18 EAST 22ND STREET.
Copyright MDCCCXCVIII in the United States of America by Francis Day & Hunter.
Telegraphic Address.
ARPEGGIO LONDON.
H.G. Banks Lith.

period especially romantic and picturesque figures. They were 'old salts' whose 'yarns' were listened to with respect. The resorts where fishing was still important, like Scarborough, Whitby, Yarmouth and Hastings were considered 'real live places', and even when the fishermen were quietly making a profit out of the visitors – charging them too much to take them out for a sail, or selling them nets to be used in suburban gardens – they seemed to have a special dignity that differentiated them from all other seaside characters. In the 1880s there was a group of artists working in Cornwall, known as the Newlyn School, who specialized in painting the fishermen – sitting on the quays mending their nets and looking wise and weather-beaten, or eating frugal meals in their simply furnished cottages with the grey, threatening waves glimpsed through the window.

Storms, and high tides and huge waves breaking over the promenade mesmerized visitors to the seaside. As enthusiastically as eighteenth-century aesthetes in search of the sublime, ordinary holidaymakers would now put on

Opposite
Marie Lloyd's song in praise of mixed bathing, which was still against the rules of most English resorts

Old fisherman and his wife at Whitby, Yorkshire Photograph by Frank Meadow Sutcliffe, *c.* 1900

their overcoats, turn up their collars and rush out into the wind to witness the violence and drama. In *Clayhanger*, published in 1910, Arnold Bennett describes a typical crowd of sightseers in Brighton watching a storm at night. 'The play went on endlessly, hypnotising the spectators who, beaten by the wind and deafened by the sound, stared and stared, safe, at the mysterious and menacing world of spray and foam and darkness.'

At the beginning of this century a series of postcards was produced showing rough seas lashing themselves against the piers and seafronts of every popular resort. They were a huge commercial success; and people even came to the seaside out of season especially to see the storms. Mill-workers poured into Blackpool when a ferociously rough sea seemed likely, and when, though the highest tide of the century had been predicted, the water was unexpectedly calm, their disappointment was keen. 'Their great tide is nowt i' th' world but an arrant sell, gotten up by lodgin' heawse keepers, an' railway chaps, and newspaper folk, an sich like wastril devils, a-purpose to bring country folk to the water side and hook brass eawt o' their pockets,' grumbled an old Boltoner who swore that he would never set foot in Blackpool again.

Crowds watching the high sea at Hastings

'Wish You Were Here...'

Looming up above the terraces, and dominating the sea-fronts of many English resorts are the late-nineteenth-century grand hotels – memorials to the prosperity of the seaside at the turn of the century. Often they were designed by men who specialized in monumental civic splendour. Sir Cuthbert Broderick the architect of one of the first of them, the Grand at Scarborough which was opened in 1867, also designed Leeds town hall; and Waterhouse built several town halls and the Natural History Museum as well as the Metropole at Brighton. Their hotels stand out from the surrounding buildings not only by their size, but also because they were usually made of quite different materials from the older and more traditional seaside buildings that surrounded them. The bright red brick and terracotta of the Metropole, completed in 1890, looks striking and aggressive among its pale surroundings, and it must have been even more startling when it still had its pointed Gothic roofs and pale green spire piercing the skyline.

By the 1890s every resort of consequence in England had at least one or two big hotels; in fact the number of them is a fair guide, if not to the prosperity of the town, at least to the status of its habitués at the turn of the century – obviously as a general rule, the richer the visitors, the more numerous the grand hotels. Not surprisingly East-bourne, Cromer and Bournemouth have lots of imposing ones. The most impressive at Eastbourne is a huge stucco mock-French château called the Grand – the English seem to be unimaginative about naming hotels – and the cliffs of Bournemouth are dotted with elaborate and varied examples.

Inside these big hotels there were often all sorts of luxuries like splendid ballrooms, Turkish baths, Moorish smoking-rooms and marble fireplaces; and as they grew

The Hotel Metropole, Cromer, built 1899

taller and taller lifts became essential. In the late 1860s when they were first installed at the Grand at Brighton these were alarming novelties and were known as 'ascending omnibuses'. Medium-sized hotels concentrated in their advertisements on the merits of their plumbing. The Pavilion at Scarborough which catered for 'the families of gentlemen', claimed that 'the sanitary arrangements are perfect having been thoroughly overhauled under the direction of the Authorities and a certificate given to that effect'.

In spite of the successful new hotels and the rows of boarding-houses, most people at the end of the nineteenth century were still spending their holidays by the sea – as they had since the eighteenth century – in lodgings, more or less self-contained rented rooms. Mr Pooter stayed in 'very nice apartments near the station. On the cliffs they would have been twice as much.'

This kind of accommodation was provided for a wide range of people from prosperous middle-class families who rented a whole house – except for the attics and basements which were the province of the landlady and her hard-worked servants – to Lancashire mill-workers who slept three or four to a bed in 'company houses' in Blackpool. The common ingredients in all these establishments were the pervading presence of the landlady and the fact that the visitors provided their own food for her to cook.

At the top end of the scale the family's servants would buy their provisions in the local shops, but generally the mother would spend some of the morning choosing freshly caught fish or buying 'made-up' delicacies from shops like Muttons in Brighton – a special seaside cross between superior grocer, caterer and take-away restaurant, a few of which still survive in a rather run-down way in select south coast resorts. Visitors often brought their own sugar and kept their tea in locked caddies, to which prudent landladies had skeleton keys; while basics like bread, flour, potatoes, butter and milk were provided. It must have made cooking horribly complicated; five or six different meals might have to be prepared simultaneously for families with vivid memories of the exact size of their joint. There were endless complaints about vanishing chicken legs, sherry and tea, and unexpected extras on the bill, 'such as knife-cleaning, proportion to the water rate, loan of latch-key, etc.'

Often each family ate separately in their own rooms, but in cheaper lodgings they would all dine together 'on the competitive principle'. At Blackpool, in an extension of the same system there was an enigmatic notice in many lodging-house windows which read 'Hot water twopence'. This meant that people could come in off the beach clutching their tea caddies and buns, and the landlady would provide teapots,

IN THE SMOKING ROOM

THE SALLE A MANGER

THE TURKISH BATH

BALL ROOM FROM THE GARDEN.

hot water, cups, chairs and tables. It was considered a
profitable sideline.

While for the middle classes, taking lodgings was a way of
ensuring privacy and avoiding undesirable company in the
dining-room, at resorts which catered mainly for the working
classes, like Morecambe, Yarmouth, Llandudno, and
especially Blackpool, the lodging-houses had tremendous
community spirit. People who lived in the same street at
home in Oldham or Preston often took over a lodging-house
for a week at Blackpool, and after a day on the beach, spent
their evenings having singsongs, playing jolly games together and making each other apple-pie beds. 'Baths and
pianos are the rule; good music and good singing are
often indulged in, coarseness or vulgarity is strictly put down,'
says a Blackpool guide of the 1890s.

Overpage
Gildersleeves Boarding
Establishment, Hastings,
c. 1900

127

GILDERS
BOARDING EST
STANTON H
PRIVATE
BOARDING
ESTABLISHMENT
GILDERSLEEVE'S
BOARDING
ESTABLISHMENT

Two postcards by Tom Browne in the 'Seaside Comforts' series, *c.* 1905

Seaside landladies might sometimes have been strict enough to put down coarseness and vulgarity in their own parlours, but they could not suppress the spate of jokes against themselves. They were seen as tight-lipped tartars filling their rooms, especially their bathrooms, with dictatorial little notices and imposing endless regulations, or as 'refeened' obsequious widows who wept if you disputed the bill, or as stout, slovenly creatures always taking surreptitious swigs of your whisky. In fact, they became all-purpose joke figures, like mothers-in-law. But they must usually have been regarded with a certain affection by their visitors, for families commonly returned year after year not only to the same resort, but to the same lodgings – friendly, secure and unchanging, but for a slight increase in the layer of sand under the carpet in the hall and some new shrimping nets propped up in the porch.

130

Victorian and Edwardian fiction is full of moans about the discomfort of seaside lodgings and boarding-houses, but perhaps complaining was part of the whole slightly masochistic pleasure of a holiday by the sea. The overcrowding, the chairs stuffed with shingle, the flies in the butter and the flypapers dangling among the souvenirs on the mantelpiece and hitting one in the eye, the boredom of Sundays when the landlady locked up the piano, the soup 'like warm table beer very thoroughly peppered', and the oppressive quality of someone else's attempts at cosy interior decoration that would not show the dirt.

But the most constant complaint was about bugs. It is striking how often the first question a visitor asked a landlady was whether there were any. 'Ony blanket-jumpers?' asks a Lancashire spark at Blackpool in a turn-of-the-century penny paperback. 'I suppose you have not any – eh?' said Mrs Melladew making a suggestion of creeping things in *Mattins and Muttons*. They can hardly have expected the answer yes; but bugs and fleas were a real plague of the seaside. Jane Carlyle emerged covered in bites after a night at Ramsgate, Mrs Bugsby was a favourite fictional name for landladies, the bathing-machines were often plastered with advertisements for Keatings.

> I'd be happy for ever down by the sea,
> But there's bugs here by thousands
> And a million flea

goes the caption of one of the many postcards that laughed off the problem. Conscientious landladies had to add to their labours the most rigorous searches. 'Every room was fiercely swept and sprinkled and watched by cunning eyes which nothing could escape, curtains were taken down, mattresses explored, every bone in a bed dislocated and washed as soon as a lodger took his departure.' (Thackeray, *The Newcomes*)

The kind of boarding-houses where all the food was provided were sometimes like Gildersleeves Boarding Establishment at Hastings, imposing as well as cosy – except for a certain matiness, scarcely distinguishable from private hotels – and they were often immensely good value. Mr Clarkson Rose, who was for many years a famous seaside entertainer and a connoisseur of boarding-houses, describes the huge breakfasts, with kedgeree, kidneys and ham; lunches of turbot, ribs of beef, apple tart and jam roll; dinners of prawns, soup, salmon, duck and trifle; all for two guineas a week at an ordinary seaside boarding-house in a Welsh resort at the turn of the century.

'Thanks to Sea View and its inmates,' wrote a typically appreciative visitor to Eastbourne, 'I had one of the

LES FANTAISISTES.

— Du coup, si les crabes nous résistent...

LILY

— Oh! y en a-t-il!

LA PÊCHE A LA CREVETTE. — CÔTÉ DES AMATEURS

jolliest and pleasantest holidays I have ever spent; Sea View is unique. It is not a hotel, and yet it gives you all the convenience and luxury of a hotel, with a relishing dash of homeliness and home comforts thrown in, as well as the extra charm of meeting *en famille*, a nice set of people who yearly visit it and make it their seaside home.'

However well fed people were in their hotels and boarding-houses, swimming and wandering around made them feel hungry, and the seaside has long specialized in portable food designed to be eaten standing up at a stall or sitting on the beach. From the beginning of the Victorian age many of the pedlars who swarmed on to the sands were selling food. There were some who concentrated on local specialities, shrimp-sellers with their wares in little pointed calico bags 'like babies' bonnets' and oyster vendors 'with a round basket, a bottle of vinegar and a dirty towel for wiping customer's hands'. Shrimps had far more prestige in the nineteenth century than they have today, and oysters far less. In Regency Brighton it was fashionable to eat quantities of shrimps for breakfast and they were considered a delicacy until the end of the century. Amateur shrimping, that most satisfying of seaside pastimes, does not seem to have become popular until about the 1870s. Before then there is no sign of those straight-ended miniature shrimping nets in cartoons and pictures of the seaside. By the 1880s however, shrimping had become a craze for children, and even for young ladies – though unlike the more earnest girls of the previous generation, they ate rather than studied their prey.

Oysters were almost as cheap and plentiful as whelks and winkles. There were stalls selling them on most late Victorian beaches and they were gulped down by the dozen. The walrus and the carpenter lugubriously consuming quantities of oysters on the sands must have seemed far less unlikely figures to Victorian readers of *Alice Through the Looking Glass* than they do to us.

In English resorts there was never quite such ceremony about eating shellfish as there was in America. Clambakes were the highlights of a holiday on the New England coast. Places like Rocky Point and Crescent Park on Narrangansett Bay were known as clambake resorts, and fleets of steamboats ran excursions to the clambake sites on the shore where feasts of corn, clams and potatoes were cooked in the Indian fashion between heated rocks. Corn on the cob and clam chowder were also traditionally eaten on American beaches, and from about 1900 that most portable of all foods the hot dog became a seaside favourite.

A great variety of sweetmeats were sold on the beaches of all nineteenth-century resorts, but the origin of that symbol of the English seaside, pink lettered rock, is obscure. In

Opposite
Shrimpers at Ostend from *Bains de Mer d'Ostende*, 1885

133

Talk about eat, I could shift a whale at Southend... That's seven dozen. Fine Natives.

At Southend. Rock. Donald McGill. 'A couple of the sweet things we get down here.'

the 1850s a 'fancy confectioner' at Ramsgate had a song about his wares:

> I have best lemon cream
> When my customer calls,
> With almond candy, rock,
> And some fine brandy balls . . .

His rock was probably a hard peppermint stick, but it had not yet acquired those enticing pink letters. The earliest rock sometimes had stripes on the surface, and later simple designs of flowers or circles in the middle, but sometime in the 1860s or 1870s enterprising small confectioners began to experiment with letters. First they made rock with girls' names running through it, and later the names of towns. It was not until the late 1880s that rock began to be particularly associated with the seaside. A list of some of the food sold on Yarmouth beach in 1897 reads: 'Chocolate creams, buns, two a penny, apples, penny a bag, Yarmouth rock, penny a box, lemonade, three pence a bottle, walnuts, eight a penny, milk, penny a glass.' On Blackpool beach at the same period a Mr Bill Muggins, dressed up in clogs and a top hat, was tossing bags of Blackpool rock into the crowds; and after the turn of the century, every popular resort in England was selling its own rock.

Salt-water taffy, which was invented when a candy stall in Atlantic City was flooded by a particularly high tide in the 1880s, is perhaps almost its American equivalent, but there is no food quite so evocative of the American or continental seaside as rock is of the English. Munching a sticky, pink piece of rock, watching the name of some resort growing or shrinking, and the letters sloping in different directions

134

with every bite, never fails to bring back memories of childhood walks along the prom and all the other long-established English holiday rituals.

Seaside souvenir shops with their variety of useless little objects always seem to have had a rather tatty air about them. Dickens remarked on it: 'In our fancy shop we have a capital collection of damaged goods, among which the flies of countless summers "have been roaming". We are great in obsolete seals, and in faded pincushions and in rickety campstools and in exploded cutlery and in miniature vessels, and in stunted little telescopes, and in objects made of shells. Diminutive spades, harrows and baskets are our principal articles of commerce; but even they don't look quite new somehow. They always seem to have been offered and refused somewhere else, before they came down to our watering place.'

By the end of the nineteenth century, making cheap, mass-produced souvenirs for the English seaside resorts had become a considerable industry. They were designed to appeal to the new crowds of holidaymakers who did not have much money to spend but who wanted a little something to bring back happy memories, brighten the mantelpiece and impress their friends at home.

Wooden souvenirs made by the firm of Smith of Mauchline

Some of the kinds of souvenirs which had been sold at the beginning of the craze for the seaside had already died out or been replaced by similar but less expensive ones. In the 1830s the wood craftsmen of Tunbridge Wells had developed the technique of end-grain mosaic, which was used to decorate tea caddies and all sorts of small pieces of furniture. They had gradually stopped producing painted wooden trinkets specifically as souvenirs. However, at the same period the firm of Smith of Mauchline began making wooden souvenirs in the tradition of painted Tunbridge Ware. As they employed more mechanized techniques their products were comparatively cheap and their 'transfer woodware' was very popular throughout the second half of the nineteenth century. At their factory in Birmingham, William and Andrew Smith turned out a great variety of objects made of smooth, pale sycamore and decorated with transfer views. Spectacle cases, thermometer stands, letter racks, darning-eggs, needle cases, miniature bathing-machines – any little trinkets that could conceivably be made of wood were manufactured by the Smiths for sale at even the most obscure resorts, as well as many inland towns. They also exported souvenirs to sell to English tourists visiting favourite resorts abroad. These were exactly the same as those they could easily have bought in England, except that the views on them were of Nice or Cannes, Dieppe or Boulogne.

No English manufacturer of ceramics specialized in souvenirs in a comparable way until the 1880s, though reputable firms that made commemorative china also continued to produce fairly expensive mugs, jugs and plates decorated with seaside scenes. The Pratt of Fenton factory developed a process of building up a colour print on earthenware by superimposing several prints of different colours, and their round pots containing fish pastes or potted shrimps with views of Ramsgate or Pegwell Bay on the lid made attractive dual-purpose seaside souvenirs.

It was in the 1880s that William Henry Goss, encouraged by his son Adolphus, who was passionately interested in heraldry, decided to produce a huge range of low-priced china decorated with the crests of towns, schools, hospitals and colleges all over England. Goss's neat little vases, jugs and historic models – Roman lamps, Bronze Age urns and the occasional oddity like the life-size facsimile of a shoe worn by Queen Victoria as a baby – are made of thin, delicate porcelain and the coats of arms are painstakingly accurate. They have a rather prim quality, an aura of self-improvement which makes them seem more appropriate as souvenirs of sightseeing bicycling tours round cathedral cities than of carefree seaside jaunts. However, all sorts of modern techniques were used to market them, a network of distributors

Opposite
Typical seaside postcards,
1900–1910

136

16 PARAMÉ. — La Plage et les Villas — LL.

Souvenir from Eastbourne.

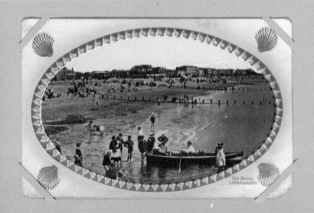

The Beach, Littlehampton

ROUGH SEA AND NEW PALACE PIER, BRIGHTON.

with exclusive territories was set up, and there was even a League of Goss Collectors, which in 1912 had nearly a thousand members, several series of Goss postcards, and an occasional magazine for enthusiasts, *The Goss Record*. Each piece sold for only a shilling or two and there were about 3,000 different crests to collect. They made Goss's fortune at a time when many other Staffordshire potteries were going bankrupt.

His success led to many imitators. Firms like Shelley, Carlton, Arcadia, Grafton and several others, including German firms, began in the Edwardian period to make cruder and jollier crested china. Unlike Goss, they tended to concentrate on the seaside market and on suitably seasidey objects like china Punch and Judy booths, Cornish pasties, busts of the popular comic character Ally Sloper or charabancs.

The most evocative souvenirs of the turn of the century were made, not in England, but in Germany, especially for the English seaside market. Many of the cheapest toys and trinkets in late Victorian England were German-made, and by the 1890s a great variety of china souvenirs were also being imported from Germany; teapots or moustache cups with a mauvish-pink lustre finish decorated with coloured scenes of Great Yarmouth or Clacton, vases embellished with gilt and pictures of 'The Promenade, Rhyl', porcelain boots with a view of Weston-super-Mare on the instep, plates with Blackpool Tower in the middle and lattice-work borders that could be threaded through with ribbon and hung up on the wall – most of them unobtrusively

Goss-type crested seaside souvenirs made by the firms of Shelley, Arcadia and Grafton, dating from 1900 to 1918

stamped 'Made in Germany'. They are perfect seaside souvenirs, desirable, useless, intricately detailed and just a bit vulgar. Their German manufacturers, as well as having the business acumen to realize the possibilities of an expanding foreign market, hit upon exactly the right style to suit it. They were particularly fond of cruets, objects which opened up all sorts of possibilities. There are innumerable pairs of binoculars, steamships with two funnels, aeroplanes and pairs of pink frilly bloomers – though no one seems then to have thought of ladies with salt and pepper in their detachable breasts.

Albums of engraved seaside views had been sold at resorts since before the Regency – they were one of the sidelines of the marine circulating libraries – and later albums with tooled leather covers containing pull-out views of all the most popular resorts became favourite souvenirs. The seaside scenes they illustrate often have an odd, surrealist look, for though the landscapes were based on photographs, the figures were generally drawn in by hand. The ladies and gentlemen strolling about are often rather out of scale. They look strangely wooden and are always

Illustration from a late nineteenth-century album of English seaside views produced in Germany

Group of Edwardian
seaside postcards

behaving with a decorum which seems unnatural when compared with the people in genuine late Victorian photographs of the seaside. It is not surprising, for these albums of views were another of the contributions of Germany to the English seaside industry, and the little people were drawn in by men who could only guess at the way holiday-makers spent their time at an English resort.

Seaside postcards – the words immediately conjure up crude, brightly coloured pictures illustrating utterly obvious double meanings of the kind eight-year-olds still find hilarious. Fat ladies leaning over the pier and 'waiting for the smacks', men with ballooning stomachs who 'can't see their little Willy', or hideous spinsters who can only swim as long as they keep 'one foot on the bottom'.

But in the Edwardian period, which was the great age of the picture postcard, this kind of rude, jolly card was only one of a huge variety of types of postcard specially designed for the seaside market. Picture postcards might have been invented for holidays – to be scribbled on the beach with cryptic messages about the weather, the journey, or just that useful phrase, 'wish you were here' – though, in fact, they were not. Their early history is complicated and obscure, but by the 1870s they were being used on the Continent for advertising, and they were soon adopted for general correspondence. The British were slow to take up the fashion. It was not until 1894 that the Post Office finally lifted most of its monopolistic restrictions and allowed cards to be sent through the post with a halfpenny adhesive stamp.

In the States souvenir postcards do seem to have made their first appearance at the seaside. In 1895 a German-American lady brought back a selection of picture postcards from Germany to Atlantic City and, inspired by them, her husband had views of the resort's piers and boardwalk printed on postcards. By 1906, one and a half million cards were passing through the Post Office at Atlantic City during August.

Their heyday in England was from 1900 to 1918, especially after 1902 when it became legal for messages as well as addresses to be written on the back of the card, allowing the picture to cover the whole of the front. The postcard publishers feverishly thought up an incredible number of novelties, and a collecting mania swept the country.

Before anyone had thought of the picture postcard, pictorial writing-paper had long been popular in England, especially at the seaside. From about the 1850s engraved views of the coast, generally taken from the same plates used for souvenir albums, were often printed at the top of writing-paper – helpfully leaving a little less room for the letter. Notepaper was also decorated with cartoons showing all sorts of seaside pleasures and disasters, many of them clumsily copied from Leech's drawings for *Punch*.

The first English seaside postcards were views, drawings and photographs, printed in monochrome; but by 1900 colour was often being used. The big postcard companies commissioned hundreds of thousands of photographs of piers and beaches, bandstands and promenading crowds, tinted them with a very restricted range of colours – the skies and water are almost always a particular washed-out shade of greenish blue – and had them printed as cards to be sold at resorts all over England. Sometimes six or seven tiny views were grouped together in a pattern, or the scene was framed with flowers, embossed shells, shrimps or lobsters. Postcard publishers like Raphael Tuck and Valentine also employed many competent artists to paint coastal scenes for reproduction; and some of the oddest inventions of the postcard craze – silk cards, aluminium cards, faked moonlight effects, even cards shaped like lighthouses, or crabs, as well as the 'rough sea' series, added variety to seaside views. Maps of resorts and their surrounding country-side were also published as postcards – an extremely useful idea; one could put them in one's pocket when going for a walk, or mark the location of one's lodgings with a cross. Many hotels provided their own postcards free as advertisements.

Pull-out cards were a seaside speciality. Concealed beneath an enticing flap in the picture was a zigzag tail of dim, micro-scopic views. These cards were usually captioned with dreadful puns: ' – is the "Plaice" for holidays' with a picture of a fish; 'All are Whelk-come at – ' with a picture of a whelk shell; 'A bottle of pop-ular views of – ' with a picture of a bottle; 'Just a line from Yarmouth', with smoked bloaters hanging up, and so on. The place-names of the Isle of Wight were particularly inspiring: 'Freshwater – you cannot drink, Lake – without water, Cowes – you cannot milk, Newport – you cannot bottle.'

Many of the cards sent from Edwardian English resorts were designed and printed abroad for sale all over Europe. Pretty children on donkeys, and bathing-beauties were international in their appeal, and German publishers produced innumerable variations on the theme of repellent men with monocles and striped bathing-costumes leering at girls through chinks in their bathing-machines. There were little beach scenes too, showing just the sea and sand, a few people and beach chairs, which could serve as a view any-where from Ostend to Eastbourne.

The first comic picture postcards published in England

were designed by established artists who had previously specialized in posters, or who had drawn for papers like *Punch* and *Vanity Fair* – men like Phil May, John Hassall, Tom Browne and Lance Thackeray. Their earliest cards explored the possibilities of new crazes like motoring or cycling; and surprisingly, it was not until they had exhausted all the jokes about these fashionable pastimes that they began to turn their attention to the seaside. Their seaside cards were far more subtle than those of their successors. All of them, but particularly Tom Browne and Lance Thackeray, drew many beach scenes, seasick families in rowing-boats, crowded lodging-houses with people sleeping in baths and chests of drawers, and trains arriving at resorts packed with trippers. These cards were the work of sophisticated graphic artists; their jokes are often good ones, their people, though comic in appearance, are not as grotesque as those on later cards, but they seem to be observing the lower-middle-class family holiday from the outside with just a touch of condescension.

Round about 1905 many unsigned, ill-drawn, crude but funny seaside joke cards began to appear, and soon Donald McGill, the great master of the rude card, started to turn his attention to the seaside. He was not at his best until the 1920s and 1930s, but his seaside world populated with hugely fat women, hen-pecked husbands with bottles of stout, sex-starved spinsters, and dumb, curvy girls, was well established by the First World War. His cards continued a long seaside tradition that went right back to Dicky Dickinson and eighteenth-century cartoons like 'The Back-Side and Front View of a Modern Fine Lady or Swimming Venus at Ramsgate'. The endearing, childish vulgarity of their humour was, and still is, an essential part of the atmosphere of popular British resorts.

More photographs must have been taken on beaches than anywhere else. All through the second half of the nineteenth century every seaside resort had at least one beach photographer. With black cloths thrown over their heads and the tripods of their cameras jammed into the sand, they shepherded innumerable families into tight groups for their holiday portraits, or got them to stick their heads through one of their jokey props and stare out over flat painted bodies.

Late-nineteenth-century resorts are particularly well documented with photographs. Before the days of postcards, many resort photographers used to fill the windows of their studios with general views of the seafront and the beach which they hoped to sell to the holidaymakers as souvenirs; and the variety and liveliness of the seaside also attracted many

Children looking through a seaside photographer's prop

143

The author's mother and aunt, *c.* 1915

serious Victorian documentary photographers, both amateur and professional. Paul Martin, for instance, who specialized in pictures of the street life of London, also photographed its seaside equivalent – city children excitedly paddling or watching Punch and Judy shows, and trippers, released from their offices and factories, relaxing on the sands; and in the Yorkshire seaside town of Whitby, Frank Meadow Sutcliffe took many extremely vivid photographs of the fishermen and fishing-boats and local children playing on the shore.

In 1900, the Box Brownie was invented and photography suddenly became cheap and easy for everybody. Millions of amateur photographers all over Europe and America began to bring their own cameras down on to the beach and take their own holiday snapshots – perhaps the most nostalgic and personal of all seaside souvenirs. Every old family album has its faded pictures of children by the sea – one's aunts and grandmothers – standing with their bare feet in the water and the sun in their eyes, smiling straight at the camera.

High Society

By the second half of the nineteenth century the English seaside resorts had become so popular with everyone else that they had scarcely any attractions left for people in 'high society'. They lacked sophistication, elegance, and above all, exclusiveness. The very rich did not have holidays, for almost their whole lives were spent in an elaborate yearly round of pleasure. Wintering on the Riviera had become an essential part of this ritual, and if they felt the need of a summer visit to the seaside, there was always Biarritz or Deauville, which became very chic after the turn of the century, or perhaps Trouville, Dieppe or even Ostend.

Scarborough or Cromer were suitable for the children. Brighton was impossible in the summer, but from November to early December, when no trippers would think of going there, it became fashionable again. Duchesses would take a house in Lewes Crescent to escape the London fogs and regain their strength before the taxing round of balls and house-parties at Christmas. They spent their time parading up and down the King's Road in their carriages. 'The beach is ignored,' wrote Richard Jefferies of these upper-class winter visitors, 'the sea is not "the thing" in Brighton, there is more talk of horses.' For about a month every year something of Brighton's grand Regency swagger and aristocratic horsiness was recaptured; and for just one glorious week in August the most elegant society in Europe descended on another much smaller English seaside town.

'Following the lead of the Prince of Wales, social England converted the regatta week at Cowes into one of the greatest social functions of the fashionable year. Society decrees that before it spreads itself over Europe in the autumn, its first taste of fresh air after the fatigues of the London season should be inhaled at the little town

Yachting in the
Mediterranean.
From *The Illustrated
London News*, 1899

on the Solent. . . . All the nicest and prettiest people in England are here,' went on the anonymous author of the snobbish little article of the 1880s, 'and the finest and fairest women of two hemispheres are lounging in wicker chairs on the Castle lawn.'

Charles II had first introduced the idea of sailing for pleasure to the English when he went yachting with his brother at Cowes, as he had in Holland during the years of his exile; but it did not become fashionable until the Regency. The Royal Yacht Squadron was founded in 1815 and in the early years of Queen Victoria's reign it had been dominated by bluff, if aristocratic, sailors obsessed with the sport but uninterested in society. When the Prince of Wales was elected Commodore of the Squadron in the 1860s the atmosphere of Cowes changed, it was 'no longer a half-civilized resort of rough sailormen, but a Court'. Members of every European royal family now came to Cowes for regatta week. Louis Napoleon and King Alphonso of Spain were members of the Squadron, and the Kaiser always made a point of taking part in the races. He strutted about the town using out-of-date slang and almost ruined the carefree pleasure of the occasion by his tactless boasting about the naval strength of Germany.

Yachting had become the favourite sport of princes and of the very rich in Europe and America, and regatta week at Cowes was the high point of the yachtsman's year.

Watching regattas was a popular seaside pastime, but at this period yacht clubs were by definition exclusive institutions. The members of the Royal Yacht Squadron prided themselves on long preventing one of the Prince of Wales' closest friends, Sir Thomas Lipton, 'the boating grocer', from becoming a member; and the New York Yacht Club, the Squadron's American counterpart, also snubbed many of the extremely rich people who wanted to join it. As J. P. Morgan said, 'You can do business with anyone, but you can only sail a boat with a gentleman.'

Yachting was now one of the great attractions of the winter season in the south of France. In 1860 a regatta was held for the first time at Cannes, and it became, as the Prince of Wales rather patronizingly put it, 'the Mediterranean Cowes'. The Prince always had his yacht sent on ahead when he paid his regular visits to the Riviera in the 1870s and 1880s, and every winter the harbours of the Côte d'Azur were full of magnificent cutters and steam yachts riding at anchor.

In the second half of the nineteenth century the Riviera resorts grew more and more grandiose. They were full of aristocrats from all over Europe, millionaires from America, and all their shady and splendid hangers-on. Spendthrift Russian princes became almost as important to Riviera society as English lords had been earlier in the century. When Lord Brougham died at a great age, the Grand Duke Michael became the centre of social life in Cannes and made it far more lavish and less respectable. As the English had done before them, the Russians built many sprawling villas in the hills above the sea, and their own churches, shaped like scaled-down Kremlins. Every demi-mondaine in the south of France now dreamed of being kept by one of the immensely rich grand dukes, and the superior pawnshops of Nice were full of marvellous Russian jewels.

There was a new magnet for these rich, exotic visitors, even more enticing than the sophisticated company and the prospect of showing off their yachts; this was the lure of gambling for high stakes. It was owing to the accident of Monaco's independence that Monte Carlo and indirectly the Riviera as a whole became synonymous with gambling at its most extravagant and dramatic. In the mid-1850s Prince Charles III of Monaco had decided to try to establish his tiny state as a health resort to rival nearby Nice and Cannes, and to include among the amenities a casino which he hoped would increase his revenue. At first the plan was not a success, but the fortune of Monte Carlo was made when the gambling concessions were taken over by François Blanc, an organizing genius. Shortly afterwards, in 1868, a railway connection with Nice was opened. In the following year the prince was getting so much money from the gamblers that he was able to abolish all direct taxation.

Monte Carlo achieved its glittering ascendancy at a time when large-scale gambling was being suppressed in most other parts of Europe. In England the Gaming Act of 1845 had effectively ended commercially organized gambling, which had never, anyway, played an important part in resort life. In France, until the end of the century when *chemin de fer* was legalized, the seaside casinos were not primarily gaming-houses but the centres of all sorts of other, more innocent entertainments. The great gaming-rooms at the German spas like Homburg and Baden had their seasons in the summer, leaving Monte Carlo free to take over their clientele in the winter, and in the 1870s they too were closed down so that temporarily Monte Carlo was without any real rivals.

John Addington Symonds described the powerful glamour of the casino in his deepest purple prose. 'There is a large house of sin blazing with gas lamps by night, flaming and shining by the shore, like pandemonium or the habitation of some romantic witch. The air swoons with the scent of lemon groves; tall palm trees wave their branches in the garden, music of the softest and most inebriating passion swells from the palace. . . . Splendid women with bold eyes and golden hair and marble columns of Imperial throats are there to laugh, to sing songs, to tempt. . . . Inside the gambling house play goes forward like a business. . . . Little can be heard but the monotonous voices of the

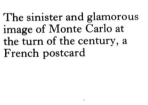

The sinister and glamorous image of Monte Carlo at the turn of the century, a French postcard

croupiers, the rattle of gold under their wooden shovels and the click of the ball spinning round the roulette.'

François Blanc realized the importance of providing all sorts of other amusements to help the gamblers spend the money they had won within the principality and to get the unwary to the gaming-tables. He organized the layout of ornamental gardens and the building of grand hotels and restaurants, and made the theatre at the casino famous for the staging of opera. The casino itself, built in 1880, is suitably alluring and ornate – a sumptuous neo-baroque palace designed by Charles Garnier, the architect of the Paris Opera House. A big bronze angel is seated on the roof and naked ladies puffing cigars float across the ceiling above the bar.

Monte Carlo came to symbolize everything opposed to the stifling bourgeois Victorian virtues. It had immense fascination even for people who could never possibly afford to go there; late Victorian magazines are full of articles about feckless aristocrats being ruined at the tables, Ouida heroines lie about on Monte Carlo balconies, and 'the man who broke the bank' became the hero of the music-halls. 'Monte Carlo', wrote Sem, the French cartoonist who drew many of the most famous gamblers at the turn of the century, 'is the high life of the great capitals of the world, condensed during the season on this splendid rock, in a fairytale of light and luxury.'

Many people still came to the Riviera in the winter for their health. Guy de Maupassant described Cannes in the 1880s as, 'the hospital of the world and the flowery cemetery of the aristocracy of Europe'. Queen Victoria, who late in life discovered the south of France, was more optimistic about the effects of the climate on her health – when she was dying she suddenly said, 'Oh, if only I were at Nice, I should recover.'

Queen Victoria utterly scorned gambling – she made a great point of snubbing the Prince of Monaco – and had little interest in yachts, but after her first visit to Grasse in 1891, she fell in love with the Riviera and returned there almost every year throughout the 1890s, staying in various hotels surrounded by a huge retinue of servants including Scottish gillies and Indian attendants. She was charmed by the landscape, and every morning went out in a donkey-cart along secluded paths shaded by olive trees, umbrella pines and mimosa. In the afternoons she would drive in her carriage along the coast roads to catch glimpses of the sea and distribute alms from her blue silk purse to the attentive beggars. Like her son (who appeared at the Battle of Flowers at Cannes in 1889 disguised as the devil in

scarlet and horns), she enjoyed all the traditional local fêtes which had by then become tourist attractions. The queen tossed carnations with such enthusiasm that footmen had to rush surreptitiously about collecting flowers that had already been thrown and returning them to her as ammunition. She also enjoyed the society of all her fellow kings and queens, for they like other rich aristocrats descended in force on the Riviera during the season – in 1890 there were sixty members of European royal families staying in Cannes.

The continental resorts of the rich were now built on the scale of capital cities rather than country towns. The hotels did not tower above their surroundings, they dictated the scale of the promenades. At Cannes, the Croisette was like a wide lop-sided Parisian boulevard with the sea on one hand and on the other an unbroken line of enormous hotels – 'Huge pretentious palaces', wrote Augustus Hare, 'which vie with each other in comfortless parade.' Some of the biggest Riviera hotels, like the Negresco at Nice and the Carlton at Cannes, were built after the turn of the century, but they had many monstrous predecessors put up in the 1880s and 1890s. Queen Victoria and her retinue stayed at four different hotels on the Riviera – her bill for thirty-five days at the Grand Hotel de Cimiez at Nice was £1,500 – and there were a great many others which were large and sumptuous enough to accommodate kings and queens.

No other resorts had quite the flashy splendour of Nice, Cannes and Monte Carlo, though several were almost as international. At Biarritz, which became the favourite of Edward VII after he had come to the throne, hunting and country-house pleasures were combined with a stately upper-class version of the family holiday. Well-brought-up children from Moscow, Paris and Berlin met on the sands and went to the children's balls at the casino. Deauville, next door to Trouville, had a fine racecourse. It had been founded by the Duc de Morny as an expensive 'summer Paris', where people could 'throw money out the windows'. Ostend was popular with all classes, but many elegant Parisians went there and smart young Englishmen crossed the Channel to enjoy the casino and the mixed bathing.

The beaches of continental summer resorts were subtly different from those in England. There were fewer pedlars, they were more spick and span, and better organized. There were often wooden boards laid over the sand like the famous *planches* at Deauville, which were imitated as boardwalks at Atlantic City and other American resorts. Strips of matting protected bare feet from the pebbles. There were rafts for diving and flags and pennants fluttering. The chairs were different. They were not just deck-chairs (which had been introduced on the P. & O. liners in the 1880s and by the

Opposite
Queen Victoria taking her morning drive at Cimiez
From *The Illustrated London News*, 1897

151

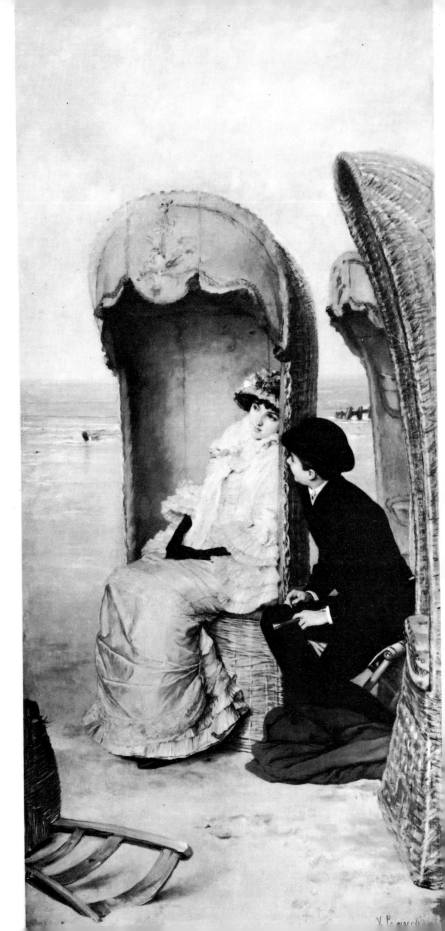

The Confession by
Vincente Palmaroli, 1883

Opposite, above
The Beach at
Boulogne-sur-Mer by
Manet, 1869

Opposite, below
On the Beach at Dieppe
by Degas, 1876–77

end of the century replaced ordinary upright chairs on most English beaches), but all sorts of local variations to protect bathers from the sun or the wind. The most striking were the huge, enveloping wicker chairs popular at Dutch and Belgian resorts. 'They are single or double,' says Bernard Becker, 'the latter being greatly in request by very young people, and are provided with a footstool; so that they are very comfortable for reading, knitting, smoking or sleeping in. They have extended down the coast as far as Ostende, where, however, they are not in great request. Probably the same reason which has prevented their adoption at Ostende has stood in their way in this country. They have every virtue it is true; but they not only shelter, but conceal the occupant. What, I should like to know, is the use of a delicious seaside toilette if madame is to be buried in the vast arms of a porter's chair? What becomes of the killing costume and the scarlet umbrella if they are literally put under a bushel?'

Only in the United States could healthy visitors to the seaside enjoy the invalid's pleasure of being bowled along beside the waves in a sort of superior bath-chair. By the end of the century riding down the boardwalk in a basketwork rolling chair, 'glowing richly under varnish' and complete with pusher, was a popular pastime at Atlantic City and other American resorts.

On all the continental beaches there were stripes everywhere – the neat rows of tents were made of canvas with bright, wide stripes, the flapping awnings were striped, and almost all the men and many of the women wore striped bathing-costumes, making a brilliant stripey dazzle in the summer sunlight.

A child lying on the beach, having her hair combed by an old nurse; two women sitting on upright chairs on the sands reading, their faces shaded by parasols, with a child's shoe drying on the back of the empty chair between them; little figures on Boulogne beach, girls, a donkey, a man with a sunshade and a woman with field-glasses watching the steamers on the horizon. In the late nineteenth century the seaside had a particular attraction for artists, and the Impressionists and the generation of painters which followed them have left us many vivid images of the beaches – images even more memorable and immediate than contemporary photographs.

The beach was a perfect subject for the Impressionists – Nature tamed a little, and inhabited by people enjoying themselves. The bright light on the water, the wide skies, the groups of women in summer dresses casually lounging or strolling about, exactly fitted in with their preoccupations.

Boudin, their precursor, was the first French artist to paint the newly fashionable seaside resorts. He began working on his sketchy, atmospheric little pictures of Trouville in the 1860s and by the 1870s he was beginning to feel slightly trapped by his success with the subject. 'I shall always', he wrote, 'be labelled a painter of beaches.' Like him, the Impressionists were attracted by the seaside towns on the Channel coast. Monet painted many beach scenes at Trouville, Manet at Boulogne and Degas at Dieppe.

Dieppe with its picturesque old town and chic modern casino had a special charm for artists. Many of the seaside pictures by the followers of the Impressionists, like Sickert and Whistler, were painted there, and by the turn of the century the town had become a haven for every slightly scandalous English aesthete. Oscar Wilde made straight for Dieppe when he was released from prison, and Beardsley loved wandering about in the casino. 'I shed bitter tears on leaving Dieppe,' he wrote when he was dying, 'I had so many nice friends there and amusing aquaintances.' Sickert lived for years in the fishing quarter and Ernest Dowson, Max Beerbohm, Conder, Whistler, George Moore, almost all the famous *fin de siècle* dandies, were habitués of the place.

In the first issue of *The Savoy* there was an article about Dieppe by Arthur Symons illustrated by Beardsley. 'What is it', he asked, 'in this little French watering-place that appeals so to the not quite conventional Englishman?' He goes on to describe some of the pleasures of sitting on the terrace of the casino. 'If you would do in France as the French do, you can sit nearer the parapet, with an awning stretched above your head, and look drowsily over the sea, which is worth looking at here, opalescent and full of soft changes; and you can chat with as many of the *beautées de plage*, Polish princes, and distinguished artistic people as you happen to know. There is the Prince de Sagan, with his irreproachable button-hole; the Comtesse de Greffuhle is standing on the *estacade*; Massenet and Saint-Saëns are sitting on chairs yonder; Cléo de Mérode, the 1830 beauty of the Opera, whose photograph you have seen in every shop window in Paris, is taking her bath, wearing the prettiest little black socks, yellow gloves, and a thin, many-twisted gold chain about her neck. All round you, bright in the bright sun there is a flow of soft dresses, mostly in sharp, clear colours, vivid yellows, and blues and whites, the most wonderful blues more dazzling than the sea. And there are delicious hats, floating over the hair like clouds; great floating sleeves, adding wings to the butterfly. I adore beautiful summer dresses, and here at Dieppe, you have all the fashions and felicities of a whole summer. . . . How many beautiful faces there were, people one never knew, and yet

The illustration by Beardsley for Arthur Symons' article on Dieppe in the first issue of *The Savoy*, 1895

L'Eté à Ostende, poster
by Tamagno, late
nineteenth century

Toilettes de plage. A fashion
plate from *La Mode
Illustrée*, 1900

meeting them at every hour, at dinner, on the terrace of the casino, at the tables, in the sea, one seemed to know them almost better than one's friends, and to be known by them just as well. Much of the charm of life exists for me in the unspoken interest which forms a sort of electric current between oneself and strangers. It is a real emotion to me, satisfying in a sense, for the very reason that it leaves one unsatisfied. And of this kind of emotion Dieppe in the season is bewilderingly abundant.'

By the turn of the century America had the beginnings of its own Riviera, a winter resort that combined gambling and glamour. This was Palm Beach which was opened up in the early 1890s. It was entirely the work of one man, Henry Flagler, who stands out among the many entrepreneurs – landowners, hoteliers, real-estate dealers, railway magnates – who played such a large part in developing and defining the character of resorts all over Europe and America. Flagler was a railroad tycoon who dreamed of taking a line to the very tip of Florida and of creating a new resort which would be irresistible to his fellow millionaires. At first Palm Beach was nothing more than a station, a chapel, a gambling-house and a hotel, but it was such a vast hotel that it would have made any of the European monsters look insignificant.

It was called the Royal Poinciana and was six stories high and, in the old American tradition, built entirely of wood. There was room for 1,750 guests, 2,000 people could sit down at once in the dining-room, and if anyone had felt the urge to pace the corridors of the hotel he could easily have walked seven miles without retracing his steps; though a double room cost 100 dollars a day the hotel was often full. Flagler had the outside of the Royal Poinciana painted a brilliant shade of lemon-yellow and as a final touch of megalomania it was made in the shape of a gigantic F.

A studied lack of ostentation was, however, far more typical of the seaside places on the East Coast where most wealthy Americans spent their summers. After the Civil War, Long Branch had become raffish, full of unsavoury people attracted by the ill-organized gambling and racing, and Cape May had declined; the rich and fastidious 'summer people' began to descend instead on thinly populated stretches of the East Coast or wild little islands. They built themselves big wooden villas with unfenced lawns and wide porches and verandahs overlooking the sea; and went back year after year, sailed, bathed and entertained each other, and turned secluded bays on Long Island, places like Southampton, or villages on the coast of Maine, into summer colonies rather than seaside towns. This sort of American resort had none of the urban look of their English and

Opposite
A middle-class, gingerbread Gothic seaside villa at Oak Bluffs, Martha's Vineyard, *c.* 1900

158

An upper-class seaside group. 'Mr and Mrs John Drew and Miss Louise Drew on the porch of "Kylami", East Hampton, Long Island, 1902'. Photograph by Byron

continental counterparts. They were made up less of hotels and lodging-houses than of scattered, countrified second homes. Even Newport, which was still fashionable, though Southerners no longer went there, was not urban in atmosphere. 'It isn't a town,' says Mr Westgate of Newport in Henry James's *An International Episode*. 'It's well, what shall I call it? It's a watering-place. In short, it's Newport. You'll see what it is. It's cool; that's the principal thing.' Away from the stifling heat of New York or Boston the summer people lived an open-air but exclusive life, revolving round private clubs and reading-rooms and private beaches.

English resorts could never be really exclusive, however many subtle means they used to discourage the kind of visitors they considered undesirable. The foreshore in England has long been technically Crown land, and in practice by far the greater part of it was and still is public. The beaches of places like Cromer and Frinton may have been too dull, and the accommodation too expensive for many people, but though local councils could make all sorts of regulations controlling the dress and behaviour of people on the beach, there was nothing to stop anyone with a correct bathing-costume and the price of a machine from bathing there and lounging about if they happened to want to. In America seaside exclusiveness could be rigidly enforced. There, and to a lesser extent on the Continent, the seashore was often only accessible to people who owned coastal property or were staying at particular hotels, and even they were often kept off the best beaches which were owned by private clubs with all sorts of strict and snobbish regulations. To be one of the few hundred people who could set foot on Bailey's Beach at Newport was the ultimate aim of millionaires with high-society aspirations.

Newport became at the turn of the century the most extravagant seaside resort in America, and perhaps the world, but in the 1870s and 1880s it typified all the expensively simple charm of the East Coast summer colonies. 'Images of brilliant mornings on lawns and piazzas that overlooked the sea; the innumerable pretty girls; the infinite lounging and talking and laughing and flirting and lunching and dining; of universal friendliness and frankness; of occasions on which they knew everyone and everything and had an extraordinary sense of ease; of drives and rides in the late afternoon over gleaming beaches, on long sea roads, beneath a sky lighted up by marvellous sunsets; of tea-tables, on the return, informal, irregular, agreeable; of evenings at open windows or on the perpetual verandahs, in the summer starlight, above the warm Atlantic.'

Henry James makes life there in the 1870s sound delightfully spontaneous and hospitable – innocent in comparison with the ancient intricacies of English society. It was in the late 1880s that a sea-change came over Newport. The new breed of multi-millionaires, the Vanderbilts, the Belmonts and the Astors, decided that it would make a splendid setting in which to display their vast wealth and lead a social life as hierarchical as anything in Europe. They began to build themselves new summer 'cottages' – incredible palaces stuffed with treasures from all over Europe, for they seem to have felt an overwhelming compulsion to surround themselves with the splendours of the past. 'In this country where everything is of yesterday,' wrote Paul Bourget, a French observer of the American scene, 'they hunger and thirst for long ago.'

William K. Vanderbilt's cottage, Marble House, a rather larger version of Petit Trianon, was completed in 1892; and as soon as it was finished, William Morris Hunt, the favourite architect of 'the 400', was commissioned to design the biggest of all the Newport mansions, Cornelius Vanderbilt's The Breakers. Ships came over from Europe with entire cargoes – dismantled rooms from French châteaux, frescoes and furniture – consigned to Mr Vanderbilt. It took only two years to finish and cost over four million dollars. At Belcourt Castle, built for Oliver Belmont, horses and cars could be driven straight into the house, the stables were as grand as the drawing-room, and the horses had initialled linen sheets and embroidered blankets.

Many other villas almost as lavish were built at the same

period. Walter Crane, the English artist, who visited Newport in the 1890s, describes them 'rising up along the coast in all sorts of weird architectural fashions and almost with the rapidity of mushrooms – Mr. Peabody told me that a house of this kind was expected to be finished in nine months.'

He also noted that Newport was the only place where he received no typical American hospitality – 'We were requested *not* to come at the luncheon hour.' This is not surprising for by then Newport was proud of the fact that it took at least four seasons before even the most desirable millionaire was considered socially acceptable.

When the magic door was at last opened, they and their families were invited to the enormous balls where everyone ate off gold plate and were waited on by innumerable flunkeys in powdered wigs, and to the motoring parties at Belcourt Castle where cars swathed in flowers raced at ten miles an hour round obstacle courses of dummy nursemaids, dogs and policemen. They could now sail in the bay on private steam yachts which cost 20,000 dollars a month to keep up, play tennis, or spend the afternoon at a *fête champêtre* for which a flock of southdown sheep and a few cows had been hired 'to give the place an animated look'. Once at a ball

'The Breakers' and Cliff Walk, Newport

the guests were all provided with buckets and spades and had to dig in a pile of sand in the middle of the room for diamonds, emeralds and rubies. It was all idiotically lavish and very short-lived.

After 1910 the great cottages were shuttered, locked up and empty most of the time, and soon they began to seem like relics from the distant past. They are still there, beautifully restored now, as bizarre as a row of dinosaurs gazing out to sea. 'There is absolutely nothing to be done with them,' wrote Henry James, 'nothing but to let them stand there always, vast and blank, for reminder of the prohibited degree of witlessness.'

The Last Day of Summer
by Charles Dana Gibson,
1896

Coney Island and Blackpool

Seaside delusions of grandeur were not the prerogative of the very rich. By the beginning of this century two extraordinary resorts, one in America, one in England, had been transformed by inspired showmen into dreamworlds where, for a day or a week, ordinary people could enjoy fantasies of excitement and luxury.

Coney Island in the 1850s had been described as, 'solitary and with a wild charm', but by the 1880s it was a sprawling resort controlled by an underworld character called John Y. McKane, and was famous for gambling, prize fights and brothels. Among the 'dens and dives' some bizarre follies had already been built, like the huge elephant described on a poster as 'The Acme of Architectural Triumphs – A Whole Summer Resort in this Unique Giant'. There were spiral staircases inside his legs and one could look out over the ocean from windows in his head or from the balcony on his back. However, Coney's bad reputation deterred respectable New Yorkers, and it was not until after McKane had been arrested in 1894 and the town had been cleared of most of its racketeers that its great period as a popular resort began. In 1897 Steeplechase Park, the first of Coney Island's amusement parks, was opened.

By the turn of the century there were many amusement parks on the outskirts of big towns. Often, they had been set up by the trolley-bus companies as a way of increasing the number of their passengers. Trams played a more important part in the recreation of most people in the States than they did in England. They did not just carry passengers from one part of a city to another, making parks and sports grounds accessible to everyone, they eclipsed the railways for all but the longest journeys – it was even possible to take the trolley all the way from New York to Boston.

The trolley-bus companies developed their seaside picnic

Poster for a typical, turn of the century seaside amusement park, set up by a trolley-bus company

A Trolley Bus Excursion. From *Harper's Weekly,* 1896

and amusement parks near crowded East Coast cities into full-scale resorts, though they were places to be visited for an evening or week-end treat rather than for an annual holiday. At Jantzen Beach, Portland, Revere Beach outside Boston and at Gravesend Beach on Long Island, they built piers and concert halls, dining-rooms, zoos and bandstands. They permanently installed bigger and grander roundabouts and rides than were possible in fairs which were always having to be packed up and moved on to a new site; and they usually made certain that there was no way of getting to their amusement parks except by trolley. On summer evenings the open cars were packed with people going to spend a few hours at the pleasure beaches.

'Wonderland, Wonderland that's the place to be,' went a song in praise of Wonderland Park at Revere Beach.

> Each night when I call on my sweetie she
>   says to me,
> 'Let's take a trolley ride to the ocean side,
> Where the shining lights are grand,'
> If you want to make good,
> As a true lover should,
> Just take her to Wonderland.

Most of these seaside parks were not particularly imaginative in the amusements they provided – Ulmer Park looks utterly prosaic in the poster; but an excursion to Coney Island in the early years of this century was an exotic experience. In the centre of New York you could board an open trolley wreathed with lights; a brass band played as you went along through the dark streets; and at the end of your journey you found yourself part of a series of splendid illusions.

'With the advent of night, a fantastic city all of fire suddenly rises from the ocean into the sky. Thousands of ruddy sparks glimmer in the darkness, limning in fine, sensitive outline on the black background of the sky shapely towers and miraculous castles, palaces and temples. Golden gossamer threads tremble in the air. They intertwine in transparent, flaming patterns, which flutter and melt away, in love with their own beauty mirrored in the waters,' wrote Maxim Gorki about Luna Park. It was, 'fabulous beyond conceiving'.

You could drift in a gondola past the façade of the Doge's Palace, ride a camel through the Streets of Cairo to 'the clashing of cymbals and the howls of Arab swordsmen', or brave two great, fiery monsters and enter 'the dragon's gorge'. You could visit an island in the Philippines complete with fifty-one head-hunting savages, watch volcanoes erupting and dams bursting, go on a trip to the moon, or stroll under an arch made by the huge wings of a naked

166

stucco goddess into Dreamland. Bands played without pause
and there was dancing all night in gilded ballrooms.

From Barnum to Cecil B. De Mille to Disneyland,
Americans have excelled at spectacular popular entertainment; Coney was part of this tradition and there was
immense conviction about all its escapism. The great
amusement parks, especially Luna Park and Dreamland, had
real glamour. After a few years they began to look shabby,
but at first it did not matter that the towers and domes were
made of plaster and not marble, they were as extravagantly
detailed and looked as lavish and baroque as any Riviera
casino.

Many of the most spectacular effects were borrowed from
the World's Columbian Exhibition which was held at
Chicago in 1893 to celebrate the 400th anniversary of the

Luna Park, Coney Island,
at night, 1903

discovery of America. Throughout the second half of the nineteenth century, international exhibitions had inspired extremely inventive buildings; the 'White City' as the Chicago Exhibition was nicknamed, was, however, the despair of *avant-garde* architects. It was a wedding-cake vision of French academicism which appealed immensely to the American public as a whole, for they, like the millionaires of Newport, were fascinated by the splendours of the past and by European sophistication. The Electricity Building, a turreted palace brilliantly illuminated with electric light, and an enormous Ferris wheel with cabs each big enough to hold sixty passengers were the exhibition's main concessions to modernity.

George C. Tilyou, the man who had led the campaign to clean up Coney Island, went to the Chicago Exhibition on his honeymoon. He at once realized some of its possibilities and brought the giant Ferris wheel back to Steeplechase where it became one of its great attractions; but it was his rivals, the proprietors of Luna Park and Dreamland who a few years later re-created and improved on Chicago's plaster and electric romance.

Tilyou's Steeplechase Park was a place for thrills, shrieks

Opposite
Strolling round
Dreamland in 1905,
with 'The Doge's Palace'
on the right

A panoramic view of
Steeplechase Park, *c.* 1904.
An oil painting by Lee
McKay who was
employed there

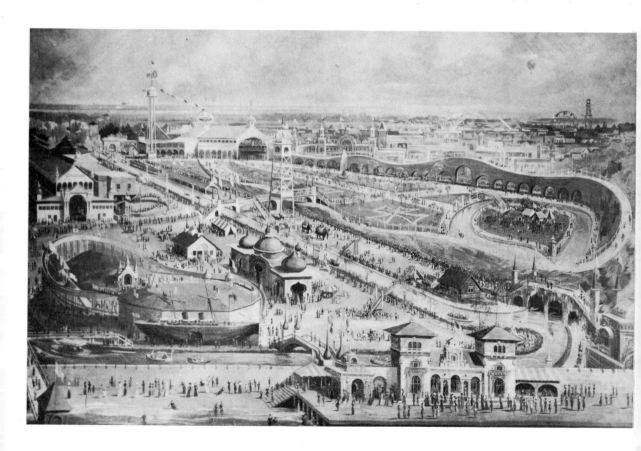

and slapstick – its famous poster advertising 'Steeplechase, The Funny Place' showed a cartoon of him grinning literally from ear to ear. It got its name from the wooden horses that took their riders zooming along a track running all round the fifteen-acre park, up and down slopes and in and out of pavilions. At the end of the track the riders passed through a dark tunnel and emerged on a small stage where, to the laughter of an audience who had gone through the same ordeal before them, they were tripped up, tickled, their skirts blew up and their hats were whisked off. One of Tilyou's most influential discoveries was that people would pay to laugh at themselves and each other.

He developed many other new inventions. There was the Wedding-Ring, a wooden ring that could seat seventy people and rocked backwards and forwards showing lots of ankle, the Barrel of Love – 'talk about love in a cottage, this has it beat by a mile', The Bounding Billows, the Blow Hole, the Human Roulette Wheel and the Razzle-Dazzle; and in the middle of all these novelties was El Dorado, the biggest and most ornate traditional carousel in America. The roaring music of its great organ reverberated through the park and out over the crowded beaches. All Steeplechase's attractions, 'everyone of them original, up-to-date and snappy', could be sampled for twenty-five cents.

Steeplechase Park was burnt to the ground in the first of Coney's great fires in 1907. The next morning, the indefatigable Tilyou put up a notice which read: 'Admission to the Burning Ruins Ten Cents.' The following year it was opened again, bigger and noisier than ever with even more titillating and thrilling diversions. But when the palaces of Dreamland were burnt down in 1911 they were not rebuilt.

Coney grew more and more crowded with day trippers after the subway reached it at the time of the First World War. It remained brash and exciting, full of oddities and inventiveness, but gradually most of its special, make-believe glamour evaporated.

'No expense spared', 'we cater for quality and we give them quality', 'the best, regardless of expense' – these were favourite Blackpool phrases, and there was a ring of truth about them.

The people who visited Blackpool always seem to have enjoyed themselves with a special north country gusto, and by the end of the nineteenth century there was a feeling of tremendous high spirits about the place. The town was packed every summer with workers from Yorkshire and Lancashire. They had a year's savings in their pockets, they were determined to have 'a reet good do' and not to waste a moment of their holiday. There were comic turns, singing and dancing in the pubs from nine-thirty in the morning till eleven at night, and dancing began on the People's Pier at five o'clock in the morning when the first trains arrived. 'Both piers were crowded,' wrote Trafford Clegg in 1891, 'breet wi' colour fro' th' women's fancy frocks, full o' stir an' bustle. On one pier th' fashionable folk swaggert thryin' to look as if they never sarved o'er a shop counter, nor gone late to th' beef market buyin' cheap cuts, on t'other were th' gradely folk lookin' like what they were dancin' as hard as they could.'

Blackpool's local impresarios, as daring and extravagant as Coney's, responded to the extraordinary energy of their customers by making a holiday there a great bargain. 'No more fun can be found for less money anywhere else in the world,' wrote the *Morning Post*. All Blackpool's entertain-

Crowds on the North Pier, Blackpool, *c.* 1910

ment buildings were extremely lavish and of an enormous size. The Winter Gardens which was opened in 1875 could hold 6,000 or 7,000 people and 3,000 people could dance in the splendid Empress Ballroom.

All the great comedians, singers and actors of the period performed in Blackpool, lured by huge fees. 'If the world be amused, startled or entertained by some new "star" in the matter of public entertainments, however distant the scene of his triumphs may be,' said a Blackpool guide in 1897, 'it can safely be predicted, that if Blackpool entrepreneurs cannot transport him to their stage, no other place in the kingdom can.' Caruso was paid £1,000 for a performance at the Winter Gardens and could only escape from the ecstatic audience by singing the last of his dozens of encores in his overcoat. Patti, Kreisler and Melba were also triumphant, and so were Marie Lloyd and Albert Chevalier; but Sarah Bernhardt, with a sore throat, was booed unmercifully, and Blondin, well over seventy, tottering along a high wire above a painted Niagara, was not an unqualified success.

There is a story about Bill Holland, the fat and dynamic manager of the Winter Gardens, that sums up the attitude of Blackpool showmen to their customers. When he told a friend that he was going to buy a 100 guinea carpet for his pavilion he got a horrified reaction. 'For the trippers! Why they'll spit on it.' Bill Holland knew better, but the remark gave him a good slogan – 'Come and spit on Bill Holland's 100 Guinea carpet.' The crowds came, but they were too impressed by the luxury and extravagance to spit.

Before Coney Island borrowed the Ferris wheel, lights and styling of the Chicago Exhibition, Blackpool had realized the relevance of international exhibitions to seaside amusements. Inspired by the most conspicuous feature of the Paris Exhibition of 1889, they built their own Eiffel Tower. It is a little shorter than the original, though it can still be seen from five miles away, and the space between its feet is not wasted, but filled in with a grand circus building. Two years after Coney's giant Ferris wheel was installed, Blackpool had one almost as big.

As at Coney, recreations of exotic places and events were popular, though the English versions do not seem to have had quite the American flair. In 1900, the last stand of Major Wilson against the Matabele was enacted nightly with 100 real Zulu warriors who also did rousing war dances; and there were terrifying lion hunts with the beasts chained to extremely flimsy looking papier mâché rocks. Bill Holland put on spectacular shows at the Winter Gardens – a mixture of ballet and variety with the most elaborate scenery – and on the sands you could ride not just donkeys and ponies, but camels as well.

Opposite, above
Railway poster of the early 1930s

Opposite, below
French bathing-beauty postcards of the 1920s

Bridlington

GUIDE FREE FROM INFORMATION BUREAU BRIDLINGTON OR ANY L·N·E·R AGENCY

Blackpool's Pleasure Beach, England's first big permanent seaside amusement park, grew out of a gypsy encampment on the South Shore. In the nineteenth century they had told fortunes there and organized side-shows, and by 1905 a helter-skelter and switchback rides had been built. In 1910 the corporation got rid of the gypsies and 'Pleasure Beach Ltd' was formed, but it was many years before its novelties and excitements could be compared with those of Steeplechase Park.

In the use of electricity Blackpool was also outstripped by its American counterpart. It did not begin to rival the magical effects of Luna Park until after the First World War, but it was a pioneer by English standards. By the 1880s the piers and the 'golden mile' were already lit by electricity and Blackpool claimed to have the first electric street trams in England. The famous 'illuminations' which extended the town's season into autumn were introduced in the 1920s. The town council was very conscious of the importance of electricity to Blackpool, and a thunderbolt to symbolize it is prominent in the town's crest, along with a 'seagull volant'.

In its talent for self-publicity Blackpool was unrivalled. It was the first resort in England to include a charge for advertising in the rates and to pay for posters which illustrated its attractions to be put up at stations in all the surrounding counties. News of every event that might conceivably make people want to go there was telegraphed to individuals and local papers all over the north. When Nelson's old flag ship was wrecked on the beach in 1897 the advertising manager – he was nicknamed Mr Blackpool and apparently looked like Father Christmas in a yachting cap – saw that every paper in England knew about it by the next morning. On one occasion he got a little carried away by his own enthusiasm, and had accusations of sacrilege heaped upon him by letter-writers to *The Times*. Realizing that the battlefield of Waterloo was much frequented by English tourists with money to spend, he rented a farmhouse there and painted 'Visit Blackpool' in big letters all over its walls.

A Blackpool souvenir showing the tower and the big wheel, *c.* 1900

Sun Worship

Sunbathing would surely seem to any time-traveller from the past, one of the oddest of twentieth-century habits. Why ever should we want to lie on the sand, almost naked and glistening with oil, being slowly toasted browner and browner? But the cult of sun worship, which began in the 1920s and has lasted till the present day, has had an immense effect on where, when and how people spend their leisure – on the whole modern development of the seaside.

There were many different, tangled reasons for this obsession with sunshine and heat, some of which began to show themselves before 1914, even before the end of the nineteenth century. By the 1880s and 1890s the sun no longer seemed as malevolent as it had to the muffled mid-Victorians. This was partly the beginning of a feminine revolution. A touch of tan would have been unthinkable for the frilly, helpless ideal beauties of Frith or Dickens, but it was acknowledged to be quite becoming to the new statuesque heroines of the 1890s. Fashionable, open-air activities like tennis, swimming and cycling meant that women were getting used to having small portions of themselves turn brown in the summer – such small portions that the effect was a little unhappy when they put on their low-cut evening dresses – but the delights of sport seemed well worth the sacrifice of an even pallor.

Men were beginning to feel that to look healthy and athletic was an asset. They do not seem to have tried to acquire a tan, but they were pleased when they did. 'I'm getting very brown at Margate,' goes the caption of a pre-First World War postcard showing a little black boy grinning. In England by the end of the nineteenth century the bronzed, weather-beaten peasant had almost disappeared from the bottom of the social scale, now no one wanted to be mistaken for a grey-faced, urban factory worker.

175

Enterprising resorts were already compiling their sunshine statistics for use as propaganda and some doctors were beginning to feel that the sun was positively beneficial to health. As early as 1880, the resident physician to the *Girls' Own Paper*, after expressing the hope that his readers had left home 'well supplied with the proper underclothing', advised them not to be afraid of sunshine. 'You cannot have too much of it. What if it does make you a trifle brown, it will purify the blood that circulates in your veins, it will calm and tranquillise the mind, and restore the roses to your cheeks that erst were so pale. I do sincerely believe that girls would be far better in health if they would make a point of leaving their parasols at home.'

On the Continent, these vague beginnings of a belief in the beneficial effects of the sun were developed into serious medical and moral theories. In 1903 the Swiss doctor Auguste Rollier opened a famous sunshine clinic in the Alps for the treatment of tubercular patients; and in Germany in the 1890s the nudist movement, which looked back to a mythical Aryan golden age of pure and pagan sun worship, began to gain enthusiastic converts.

Already before the 1920s artists began to be fascinated by the primitive and barbaric; and indirectly this growing interest must have had some effect in making heat seem exciting and dark skin desirable. African art influenced the Cubists, jazz was beginning to be heard outside the negro ghettoes of the South and Diaghilev's Russian ballet with its brilliant sets of clashing purples and hot oranges was already influencing fashion and decoration.

J. G. Weightman in his article for *Encounter* on 'The Solar Revolution' points out that as early as 1897 André Gide was describing the pleasurable sensations of exposing the body to the sun, and in his *l'Immoraliste* of 1902 the hero sunbathes naked. Later D. H. Lawrence spelled out sunbathing's sexual implications: 'Luxuriously she spread herself so that the sun should touch her limbs, fully, fully. If she had no other lover, she should have the sun . . .'

On the eve of the First World War, all the gilded foreigners who spent their winters on the Riviera still left the coast before the beginning of May; but after 1918 a few intrepid aesthetes, mostly American and English expatriates, began to go there in summer; not to the famous resorts, but to little coastal villages, emptied in the heat of everyone except the natives. Gerald and Sara Murphy were two of the pioneers who introduced the pleasures of Cap d'Antibes in summer to their artist and writer friends. Fitzgerald, Hemingway, Léger and Picasso stayed with them there in the early 1920s. The Murphys were a charming American couple, the originals of Dick Diver and Nicole in Scott Fitzgerald's

Opposite
The Bather by Van
Dongen, 1920

176

Tender is the Night, and their life-style in the south of France inspired many imitations. Their villa, the Villa America, was one of the first houses in France to have a flat roof for sunbathing; Gerald Murphy's 'functional' dress – a sailor's striped tee-shirt, shorts and espadrilles – soon became the standard Riviera resort wear, and his wife was probably the person who started the 1920s craze for wearing pearls on the beach. Fitzgerald describes her as Nicole with 'her brown back hanging from her pearls'.

Other literary and artistic bohemians began to make for the Riviera in the summer, escaping to a life of freedom, heat and colour far from the philistinism and conventions of home. Among them were Lawrence, Katherine Mansfield, Huxley, and Isadora Duncan, who met her death in the south of France, strangled by her own scarf on the Promenade des Anglais. Colette was one of the first French writers to appreciate the flavour of the south of France in summer. She wrote lyrically about the sensuous pleasures of her new simple life at St Tropez. By the early 1920s most serious painters seem to have felt that the beach had been exhausted as a subject, but Matisse, who lived in Nice throughout the decade, and Bonnard, who had a house at Le Cannet, painted many Riviera interiors pervaded by a feeling of heat, with the blue sea visible beyond a balcony and brilliant light filtering in through shutters or striped awnings.

By the middle of the 1920s bright young things were following the artists and their hangers-on to the south of France in the summer. They dashed along the Corniche in open sports cars, drank strange cocktails, danced all day or lay grilling themselves on the rocks and playing back-gammon. New summer casinos were built – the one at Juan-les-Pins was opened in 1924 – and the harbours were now more crowded with splendid yachts in July and August than they were in February.

Swimming had never before played much part in Riviera life, but now the beaches were improved and new, glamorous swimming-pools were built. The smartest of all places to bathe was the Eden Roc Swimming Club which functioned from mid-June to mid-August and was soon taken over by the Hollywood film colony. By 1930 the Riviera seasons had been completely reversed. The summer was for the young and sophisticated, the winter only for the elderly.

A few other seaside resorts in the south began to be extremely smart, particularly the Lido at Venice which had an immense vogue. 'It was in the early twenties that some-thing happened to the Lido', wrote a journalist in *Fortune*, 'that changed it from a pleasantly smart Adriatic beach to The Place – magnet for the celebrities of two continents, perhaps the best-known beach in all the world. Just what that

Opposite
Eden Roc from *The Sketch*, 1932. 'We publish so many portraits of the patrons of Eden Roc, the Riviera bathing and basking paradise, that it's only fair to give the place itself a look-in for once. This photograph gives a good idea of what it's really like, and shows the swimming-pond, the diving-boards, the famous orange mattresses, and how the population is distributed among them. Backgammon is in progress in the foreground.'

The Lido from *The Sketch*, 1931. 'Posed on a specially built "set" of sand Mr Messel, Mme Lucien Lelong and M. Serge Lifar'

something is remains an argument. Some say it was nothing more complicated than world boom, some say Fascism. And some insist it was just plain Elsa Maxwell.' In 1925 Elsa Maxwell had been employed by an enterprising mayor of Venice to put her talent for publicity and party-giving at the service of the Lido, and this does seem to have marked the beginning of its great social success.

Soon Lido summers had a legendary chic. 'Everybody' was there, bathing and sunbathing and putting on impromptu ballets on sets made of sand. Cole Porter did press-ups outside the enormous Hotel Excelsior, Cecil Beaton raced along the sands every morning in a fez. Young things lay about displaying their brilliant beach-pyjamas and eating fresh green figs. There were 'posses of princesses', and treasure hunts, and gossip, and Noel Coward wrote a world-weary song about it all.

By the beginning of the 1930s symptoms of sun worship were everywhere. The rising sun had become a favourite theme of commercial artists; it turned up all over the place, on suburban garden gates, shoes and cigarette cases, and the stepped shapes of the temples where the ancient Aztecs had worshipped their sun gods inspired the design of millions of fireplaces and wireless sets; nudism was taken up by left-wing intellectuals; and cactuses, transplanted from the desert, seemed suddenly the most desirable of house-plants.

In defiance of the weather, the English resorts tried hard to imitate Venice and the south of France. The West Country became the Cornish Riviera, and George Landsbury opened Landsbury's Lido on the Serpentine for mixed bathing and sunbathing. Resorts all round the English coast held carnivals and battles of flowers which tended to lose their spontaneous southern gaiety in the drizzle. 'King Carnival is here,' cried the programme of Brighton's carnival in 1923. 'Thrust off your conventional garb, dress as you have never dressed before.'

The only really distinguished building put up in an English seaside resort between the wars was Eric Mendelsohn's De La Warr Pavilion at Bexhill, which was built in 1934. It was far too elegant and sophisticated for its setting, but its flat roof and wide curving sun-decks were characteristic of many buildings in the 1930s. Even in England all the most aggressively modern, functional houses and blocks of flats had flat roofs for sunbathing.

The most important new amenities constructed at English resorts in the 1920s were open-air swimming-pools. Many resorts built extremely grand ones with sun-terraces and high-diving boards. Blackpool had one of the earliest and biggest. It was opened in 1923 and cost £100,000. This reflected the new popular interest in swimming. Men now all tried to do the crawl, imitating handsome Johnny Weissmuller who broke record after record before going on to become Tarzan; and many women began to excel at the sport. In 1926 Miss Gertrude Ederle knocked two hours off the best male record for swimming the Channel and by 1928 six more women had swum across and the whole phenomenon had become rather a joke. The summer issues of *Punch* that year are full of dripping Channel swimmers.

By 1928 the most fashionable women's bathing-costumes had lost all suggestion of a skirt and stopped short at the very top of the legs. 'Jantzen – the suit that changed bathing to swimming' was an advertising slogan of 1929, and their trademark, a lythe, bathing-capped diver is the epitome of sporting, late-1920s girlhood. (Those tight rubber bathing-caps which neatly covered bobs and shingles replaced scarves wound round the head. Rubber was everywhere on inter-war beaches. Girls tossed big striped rubber balls about and hugged huge inflated animals in the water.) While women could at last wear swimsuits which were really suitable for bathing and sunbathing, men, oddly enough, were forced by local regulations at most English resorts to wear bathing-costumes known as 'university regulation suits' which were more covered up than those which their fathers had been allowed to wear.

The first sunbathers in the south of France had spread olive oil on their skin to stop it turning scarlet in the sun, but by the early 1930s the international cosmetic houses were selling special creams and lotions for the purpose. Cyclax produced Sunburn Lotion and Beauty Bronze and Helena Rubinstein's Sunburn Oil was advertised as being 'as essential as your swimsuit or tennis togs. Keep a bottle

The cover of the programme for Brighton carnival, 1923

The De La Warr Pavilion, Bexhill, designed by Eric Mendelsohn, 1934

OR THE SWEET DALLIANCE OF THE LIDO—

"HOW D' YOU LIKE MY NEW COSTUME?"
"VERY PRETTY AND FEMININE AND ALL THAT, BUT I SHOULD HATE TO BE HAMPERED BY SKIRTS MYSELF."

Cartoons for *Punch*, 1928

in your club locker and another in your beach bag.' Tanning was still such a new activity that there was a slight confusion about its vocabulary. To be sunburnt meant to go a desirable dark brown, not, as it generally does now, to peel and go red. If the sun did not shine and one could not afford to go to the Riviera, sun ray lamps could be hired or used at beauty salons, and the new, round, white-rimmed sun glasses helped the illusion.

A tan had become the symbol of modernity and sophistication. In *Private Lives*, which was first produced in 1930, Sybil and Victor reveal their inner dowdiness by hating sunburnt women – 'It's somehow, well, unsuitable' – while Amanda, the Gertrude Lawrence part, and Elyot, played by Coward himself, establish at once how alike and how chic they are by both insisting on sunbathing. 'I'm absolutely determined, I've got masses of lovely oil to rub all over myself . . . When I'm done to a nice crisp brown you'll fall in love with me all over again.'

In the States, the lure of tropical sunshine and dreams of a quick killing on the property market led to a boom in Florida. 'Florida is bathed in passionate caresses of the southern sun. It is laved by the limpid waves of the embracing seas, wooed by the glorious Gulf Stream,' went one of the spates of real-estate advertisements. Many new resorts sprang up in the early 1920s where once there had been only swamps and alligators. Flagler at Palm Beach had demonstrated how attractive Florida could be to the rich, and his railway had made it accessible. In 1915 the City of Miami Beach had been incorporated and another millionaire, Carl G. Fisher, set about turning it into a residential resort. Hotels and houses were rushed up and high-pressure advertising was used to attract buyers. Fisher employed bathing-beauties, elephants and retired hot-gospellers, and was said to 'rehearse the mosquitoes till they wouldn't bite till after you'd bought'.

In 1921 George Merrick· began constructing a new resort city called Coral Gables. It was to be the embodiment of an aesthetic vision – 'rich and full of pleasantries'. In a book called *The Miracle of Coral Gables* which he wrote under the pseudonym of Rex Beach, Merrick described himself as, 'a dreamer, a man whose eyes made pictures when they were shut; a man who beheld a stately vision and caused it to become a reality . . . too modest,' he added, 'and too absorbed in his own work to feel very much pride in anything except its success.' At Coral Gables he aimed at an atmosphere of romantic southern languor, with dripping vegetation, Venetian canals and wide boulevards. 'Fancy moonlight on a Florida lagoon; palms, black against the sky;

Taking sun-bathing seriously. Members of the Miami Biltmore County Club Sun-Tan Club enjoying a daily hour of sunshine supervised by a doctor and attendants

183

night fragrant with the salt breath of the sea and your electric gondola out of juice! You and your girlfriend should worry.'

In the States the new feeling for the exotic took the form of a passion for everything Spanish. This made sense in Florida, as it did in southern California; Cuba and Mexico with their authentic Spanish buildings were so near. At Coral Gables the houses were all Spanish in inspiration. Their roof tiles were 'torn from crumbling Cuban convents and ruined haciendas'. Merrick also acknowledged the romantic influence of the Chicago World's Fair. 'Here in Florida', he wrote, 'is growing a World's Fair city in concrete, made to live in; a mirage turned to stone and framed in a setting of tropical loveliness.' His dream town danced to Paul Whiteman's famous band playing *When the Moon Shines on Coral Gables*.

It was in Palm Beach itself that the wildest Florida architecture blossomed. It had a new lease of life at the beginning of the 1920s under the exuberant influence of Addison Mizner, an architect and real-estate operator. He

House at Coral Cables

184

filled it with vast, fanciful mansions. Like the houses at Coral Gables, they were predominantly Spanish in inspiration, but Mizner did not hesitate to add a mixture of Moorish, Gothic, or any other style from the past that caught his fancy. He always insisted on giving his buildings an instant patina of great age. Men in hobnailed boots walked up and down staircases while the cement was setting to suggest the wear and tear caused by the spurs worn by the Knights of Castile; he sprayed his new frescoes with condensed milk and then rubbed them down with steel-wool, gave his banqueting halls soot-baths to simulate the effect of centuries of candles and open fires, and attacked the masterpieces of his stone-masons with a hatchet. In spite of all their eccentricities, every millionaire wanted a Mizner mansion, and Palm Beach eclipsed Newport as the place for extravagant displays of wealth. In Europe too it became synonymous with seaside sophistication. There is a Palm Beach at Cannes with a summer casino and an art deco swimming-pool, and there are Palm Beach ballrooms and private hotels in several English resorts.

Land speculation in Florida reached such a pitch that people eagerly bought building lots that did not exist or that turned out to be deep under water. The new resort city of Boca Raton was advertised as 'The Riviera, Biarritz, Mentone, Nice, Sorrento, the Lido, Egypt – all the charms in each of these finds consummation in Boca Raton', when in fact it was scarcely more than a half-finished hotel in a swamp.

By 1925 cunning speculators began to pull out before it was too late. 'Have-Faith-in-Florida Clubs' were set up by nervous investors, but in 1926 the bubble finally burst. Merrick and even Addison Mizner were ruined, a tropical hurricane inundated Miami Beach, and the roofless grand hotels were left to the seagulls. It was the end for the time being of one of the oddest episodes in the history of seaside resorts.

In the years between the wars, in spite of slumps and depressions more and more people in both Europe and America could afford to take holidays. In England by 1939 nearly 13 million workers were entitled to holidays with pay. On fine summer days the sands of Southend or Blackpool, Coney Island or Santa Monica were often black with people.

The amusements provided by the popular English resorts were much the same as they had been before the First World War; and much of their Edwardian jollity still survived. Some of the pedlars and entertainers who had contributed so much to the animation of nineteenth-century beaches were being swept off the sands by local regulations, but there were

Overpage
Blackpool beach photographed from the tower, August 1933

185

other newer entertainments. The piers were crowded with ingenious slot machines, one-armed bandits, 'mutoscopes' and pin-tables, and they spilled over into amusement arcades. Far more cinemas were built at seaside resorts than at comparable inland towns, and many permanent amusement parks, pale imitations of Blackpool and Coney, were built along the coast.

By the 1920s the Victorian system of taking lodgings by the sea, with each family providing their own food for the landlady to cook had more or less died out. Now most boarding-houses were 'all-in' establishments, but a growing number of them provided just bed and breakfast and thrust their visitors out into the town from nine till six whatever the weather. They had to eat at fish and chip shops, pubs, or the new chains of tea-shops that were springing up all over the country. For treats there were ice-creams in tall, conical glasses, and drinks of fizzy pop at ice-cream parlours.

Very few new grand hotels were built at the seaside in England in the 1920s and 1930s, and many of the people who would have stayed in the Edwardian ones were now going abroad in search of the sun, but the family hotels increased and prospered. How sedate they were, with wicker chairs on the loggia, maids in black dresses and frilly caps and aprons serving afternoon tea on the lawn, and gentle games of clock golf.

There were, at this period, few effective controls on building, and rashes of bungalows and chalets broke out on the outskirts of resorts and on many empty stretches of coast. Some of the new unplanned developments like Peacehaven or Jaywick were without proper roads or services and had a disastrous effect on the landscape, but individually the cheaply built cabins and converted railway carriages that appeared among windswept sandhills sometimes had the merit of character, even charm. They are seaside follies on a small scale. The name painted on an eccentric wooden chalet, a relic of the 1930s that stands on the edge of a bleak Sussex beach, sums up their quality. At first glance it has an incongruous Regency flavour, the letters seem to spell 'Thistle Dome', but on closer inspection it proves to be 'This'll do me'.

Holiday camps reached the peak of their popularity in the 1940s and 1950s, but it was in 1936 that Billy Butlin, a born showman who had made his money out of amusement parks, set up the first 'Luxury Holiday Camp' in England at Skegness. The camps were always extremely good value, well-known entertainers performed there and all sorts of amenities, like swimming-pools, fun-fairs and dance halls were included in the modest sum for a week's stay which was within the reach of many working-class families.

"Are there good seats on the promenade?"

Of the "Bottomless Sea" the poets sing
But down here we've got quite a different thing

THIS IS SENT 'SOLELY' BECAUSE WE MISS YOU.

Donald McGill postcards
of the 1920s and 1930s

Happy campers at
Butlin's Camp, Skegness,
in 1936

The second camp was set up at Clacton in 1937 when the
government was considering legislation on holidays with pay,
and Butlin used as his slogan: 'Holidays with Pay –
Holidays with Play. A Week's Holiday for a Week's Wage.'
The camps were particularly valuable for families with lots
of children. They were looked after and amused while their
parents relaxed. In England children have long been expected
either to accompany their parents on holiday, or to stay at
home with them if they could not afford to get away.
By the 1920s the Colonies de Vacances in France and
summer camps for children in the States were well
established, but separate holidays for children, in spite of
school trips and scout and guide camps, have still to become
a widely accepted part of English life.

The famous Butlin heartiness was at its peak in the early

days of the camps. Billy was 'Mr Happiness', holidays were 'jollydays', the Redcoats bustled about organizing and getting everybody to join in. Meals would be interrupted by their merry cries of 'hi-de-hi', to which campers were expected to answer in unison 'hi-de-ho'. Here is a verse of the *Butlin Buddies Song* written in 1936.

Leave your shop or factory, your office or your home,
Give yourself a holiday beside the shining foam,
Come on all you scholars now and put away your studies,
Come and join the happy band that's known as
   Butlin Buddies,
Hi-ya fellers, we are Butlin Buddies.

The perennial rivalry between resorts seems to have intensified in the inter-war years. The increase in the number of motor cars meant that visitors were often no longer stuck in one resort for their whole holiday but could drive off down the coast comparing beaches and amenities. The charabanc became a favourite means of transport for those who did not have cars. They were cheaper, matier and more flexible than trains, and many groups, from pub darts teams to Sunday schools, hired them for a day's outing to the sea.

This was the great age of seaside advertising in England. The railway companies and the resorts themselves commissioned innumerable posters. Royal Academicians painted bold, deceptive views of the coast, or elegant visitors out on the golf course or playing tennis. The most famous of all English seaside posters, John Hassall's 'Skegness is So Bracing' with its jolly, bouncing Old Salt, had appeared in 1909. No one else produced such a memorable comic symbol for a resort. In the 1920s, poster designers stressed instead the mad gaiety of the most unlikely places, or their historic associations — pirates were very popular. As the 1930s progressed there was more and more emphasis on sunshine; sunbathing girls smiled from station walls, the water took on a brilliant sparkle, and at the slightest provocation the sun became part of the slogan, as in 'Eastbourne the Sun-trap of the South'.

Postcard by Donald McGill, 1923

We're stopping here - for the present!

191

Back to Nature

In the Second World War troops fought over the beaches of the Continent, while in England barbed wire festooned the promenades and mines were buried in the sands. The piers along the Channel coast had their middle sections dismantled in case the Germans might think of using them as landing-stages; and among the fleet of small boats which set out to rescue the soldiers marooned at Dunkirk, there were many seaside 'Skylarks' that never returned. Bombs made holes in the terraces overlooking the sea, and buddleia sprouted from the ruins of innumerable private hotels. It must have seemed as if the seaside would never recover.

But two or three years after the end of the war, the British resorts were playing their traditional role again; though it was in rather a muted way, in keeping with the general atmosphere of austerity. And by the beginning of the 1950s middle-class English families were once more spending their holidays abroad. Usually, as currency restrictions prevented them taking much money, they went to the nearest foreign seaside towns, old favourites in Normandy or Brittany.

It was in this period of lull before the beginning of all the new developments of the seaside in the post-war years that Jacques Tati made *Monsieur Hulot's Holiday*, a film which, besides being very funny, evokes better than any other the pleasure and tedium of the traditional seaside holiday. Tati mimed his way hilariously through a series of misadventures on the beach of a tiny resort in northern France, causing havoc at the awful hotel dances, on motor-car outings and among the gala evening fireworks.

During the drab 1940s and early 1950s sun worship was temporarily almost forgotten, but it was soon to return with more devastating effects than before. Already the bikini era was beginning. In the 1930s bras and shorts had some-

Opposite, above
Souvenirs made in Germany for the Edwardian English market

Opposite, below
Some typical scenes from English resorts

193

times been worn on the beaches, but now navels could be revealed. This was considered the ultimate in exposure – nobody then foresaw the possibility of toplessness – and the new swimsuits were named after another ultimate, an early atomic explosion at Bikini.

After the war, ordinary Frenchmen at last began to flock to their own Côte d'Azur every August. An ever-increasing number of them camped near the beaches in orange or dark blue tents; one million French people were taking camping holidays in 1950, and the figure had risen to well over five million by the early 1970s.

Many old resorts like Le Touquet or Deauville still retained much of their soignée, inter-war elegance, but the urge to get back to nature and complete informality on holiday became increasingly widespread in France. It had its most striking expression in the success of the Club Méditerranée.

The club was formed in 1951, and its camps, inspired by primitive Polynesian settlements, were set up in deserted stretches of the Mediterranean coast, in Tunisia, Morocco, Turkey and Yugoslavia, for instance, as well as in France. The holidaymakers stayed in round grass huts near the beach; newspapers, radios and neck-ties were banned and virtually no money changed hands in the villages – drinks were bought with beads. There were huge, delicious meals, open-air dancing, *le sport*, and a camaraderie normally quite alien to modern French life. The formula worked, and the attempt to re-create a primitive utopia attracted more and more people. The club has now grown and diversified, but the ambience of its villages is still much

St Tropez

the same. 'Vous êtes cordialement invité à la grande fête du soleil', says the front of a recent brochure, which is illustrated with glamorous photos of the sun scorching down, empty stretches of sand and the dark blue sea.

In the late 1950s a new resort captured the imagination of a wide public. In 1956 Brigitte Bardot was directed by Vadim in her first film *Et Dieu Créa la Femme*. It included a pioneer nude sunbathing scene and was made on location at St Tropez, which was then still a pretty, not particularly fashionable fishing village. Both Bardot and St Tropez became cults with the new generation of French youth. She bought a villa there, and the little town was filled every summer with smoothly bohemian young men and pouting blonde imitation Bardot girls and *Paris-Match* photographers taking pictures of the *séances de bronzage* with telephoto lenses. By the beginning of the 1960s St Tropez had become a sort of French Chelsea by the sea, and its vogue must have helped to change the popular ideal image of the seaside.

Ever since the eighteenth century when the owners of 'parks and good houses' quit them for 'fishing holes', the romantic appeal of the simple life has always been one of the elements in the attraction of the seaside, but now more and more people, in Britain, as in France, began to want the sea and sun without all the traditional urban trappings of old-established resorts. Tents and grass huts were a little extreme, but everyone could daydream happily of lying on the beach of a colourful fishing village. Since about the mid-1950s reproductions of particularly garish oil paintings of sunny anonymous fishing villages have been hugely popular – you can even do them yourself by numbers. They hang, conjuring up ideal holidays, in millions of suburban English sitting-rooms – often alongside that other enduring image of seaside romance, white horses galloping through the wild waves. But one of the ugly paradoxes of the modern development of the seaside is that we have killed the thing we love, and now along the coast of Spain, Italy or Yugoslavia rows of concrete boxes stand at the edge of the sea, where only ten or fifteen years ago the dream fishing villages really existed.

Inclusive package holidays by charter flight are now so much part of our lives that it is hard to remember what a recent phenomenon they are. In the early 1950s they were only just beginning, and it was not until the 1960s that there started to be really cut-throat competition between the operators of the new mass tourism. By then hotels were springing up in more and more remote places to accommodate all the new holidaymakers. They often brought economic prosperity to poor regions, but also an insidious

La Grande Motte

neo-colonialism. Along the Mediterranean coast of Spain, whose economic revival depends largely on tourism, the uncontrolled sprawl of development now seems unstoppable. Soon rows of tower blocks will stretch all the way from Almeria to Algeciras.

The new high-rise resorts like Benidorm and Lloret de Mar give tourists the basic essentials of a modern seaside holiday – the four Ss after which one of the package tour firms takes its name – sun, sea, sand and superjets. The buildings are huge and high, not so as to give the city scale and sophistication, which was the aim of many nineteenth-century resorts, but just to cram in as many foreigners as possible with views of the sea.

196

Package holidays have the great and obvious advantages of minimizing both trouble and expense. All the legendary farce-material disasters like double bookings, half-built hotels and firms suddenly going bankrupt do not outweigh these advantages from the point of view of the consumer. More British people now go on holidays abroad by charter flight than by all other methods of transport put together, including scheduled airlines; and over a third of all holidays taken abroad by the British are now spent in Spain or Majorca, the most popular of package tour destinations.

In spite of all their imports from abroad, the eggs and chips, beer and cups of tea, the drugstores, discotheques and knobbly knees contests, Spain's high-rise resorts, or at least their promoters, still sometimes like to imagine that they are undiscovered fishing villages. In the brochures the pictures of the beach at Benidorm tend to be cut so as not to include the concrete hotels that loom over it, and there is always a photo of the only corner of Lloret de Mar that is still old and pretty. Local colour, in the form of flamenco dancers and guitars, is still considered a necessity and the solitary seaside romantic in us all is ensnared by the covers of the package tour brochures. Almost without exception they show either a tanned girl on an empty beach smiling up at the sun, or an idyllic couple, hand in hand, with the sea entirely to themselves.

Some of the new seaside developments built since the mid-1960s in the south of France, Portugal and Sardinia, for instance, have profited from the bad example of the Costa Brava and tried to avoid its hideous sprawl. Only one of them, La Grande Motte, near Montpellier, aims at an atmosphere of urbanity. Its apartment blocks that surround a yacht basin are ziggurat-shaped, and recall those ancient temples to the Aztec sun gods that were such an inspiration to the interior designers of the 1930s. But the traditional fishing village has been the direct inspiration of most of the new developments that make any claims to aesthetic merit. In Sardinia, the Aga Khan built one at Costa Smeralda for the very rich, and the Forte Hotel Village provides the same sort of mock-primitive charm for the mass market. The architect of Port Grimaud, Francis Spoerry, is as keen on instant age as Addison Mizner was at Palm Beach. The roof-tiles of his 'Venice on the Var' were all hand-made so that they would soon be covered by moss. Port Grimaud is already almost more picturesque than St Tropez itself only a few miles away down the coast.

Power-boats zoom through the water, beach-buggies roar over the dunes, millions of plastic-bottomed yachts are moored in regimented rows in marinas; the seaside, especially in the States, has become a favourite setting for the display of gleaming status symbols. The coastline of America is now exceedingly valuable real-estate. More and more people want to have a private bit of beach as their backyard; but even in Los Angeles, the 'beach city', where the freeways can get you to the coast in minutes, many middle-class family houses have their own pools. For bathing – a pastime that does not require consumer durables – the sea is no longer necessary. At Miami Beach, the vacationers scuba-dive and water-ski and dash about in boats, but fewer and fewer of them spend much time on their holidays just lying on the sands and swimming in the calm sea – with 1,251 private pools in the place, it is not surprising.

In America, it is mostly the young who are hooked on the

Power-boat racing at
Miami Beach

198

The following text appears on the album cover within the image:

BEACH BOYS

MFP STEREO 5235

DO YOU
WANNA DANCE?
GOOD TO
MY BABY
HELP ME,
RHONDA
PLEASE LET
ME WONDER
DANCE
DANCE DANCE
AND OTHERS

The Beach Boys –
surfing pop

primitive, lotus-eating seaside image. They concentrate on a form of display that only needs skill and one cheap, unmechanized piece of equipment. On the California coast a whole beach culture has grown up around surfing. It began in the late 1950s when a new kind of board made of fibreglass and plastic foam began to be mass-produced. The wooden boards which they replaced had been used since surfing was first brought from Hawaii to California at the beginning of the century. They were heavy and unwieldy, and had restricted the sport to a few specialists.

The surfers are the new noble savages, obsessed with their mastery of the huge Pacific waves. They unite themselves with the forces of Nature in a way the Romantics might have envied. Their streamlined, decorative Malibu boards are their great pride and their most important material possessions. They have their own slang – almost a language – and in the early 1960s they developed their own pop music. The Beach Boys sang about *Surfin' U.S.A.* and the *Lonely Sea*.

The beaches of the West Coast seemed to symbolize freedom to other groups in the 1960s. Hippies took over Venice in California or followed Henry Miller to live in shacks in the hills over Big Sur; and Flower Children and Jesus

Freaks and meditating gurus often conducted their new rituals on the edge of the Pacific Ocean.

In England now, the most popular part of the country for seaside holidays is the south-west, the area where there are fewest old-established seaside resorts; and perhaps much of the great appeal of Cornwall lies in their very absence. The beauty of its rocky coast and its warm climate are part of the attraction, but so are the picturesque little towns like St Ives, with steep streets and artists and fishermen – English versions of the Mediterranean fishing village ideal. You can even surf-ride the mild Cornish waves.

The crowds driving to Devon and Cornwall now often stay in caravans parked in ranks on the cliff tops. The caravans may look ugly, but they free the holidaymakers from the restrictions and expense of boarding-houses and hotels. The wish to cater for oneself and the urge for independence and family privacy that went with the Victorian system of renting seaside apartments has returned in a new form; though now it is the mother and not the landlady who does the cooking. Holiday camps, recognizing the trend, are putting new kitchens into their chalets and closing down their communal dining-rooms.

The old-established English seaside resorts have tried to diversify their role. Party conferences and businessmen's conventions fill the grand hotels and floral halls. Some seaside towns have become residential havens for commuters, a few have welcomed new industries, and the population of almost all of them has become increasingly elderly. When the season is over, old age pensioners live in the boarding-houses and private hotels, and the new

Modern seaside souvenirs

bungalows on the outskirts are sold to retired people who have pulled up their long-established roots to spend their last years by the sea.

In spite of all the change and decay most English seaside resorts are still very much alive. They may be shabby and rather dowdy, but their unique architecture set against the sea – stucco terraces, Edwardian hotels, curly ironwork, wooden beach-huts – is still, on bright days, peculiarly pleasing. They are extraordinarily conservative places, living museums of popular taste at its jolliest and least self-conscious. Much of their past confidence and animation has vanished, but there are still often donkeys and Punch and Judy on the sands. They sing the old songs and tell the old jokes at the end of the pier and the brass bands play the old rousing tunes as well as selections from *The Sound of Music*. The postcards and souvenirs are a little cruder, but in spirit they have not changed much. Gaudy false teeth and dummies, and pink, sticky rock are still sold at the sweet shops, and on Brighton Pier there is even someone still cutting silhouettes. Customs and attitudes that would have died out in any other setting seem preserved by the sea air.

Most English people still have a special, rather grudging

Photograph by Tony Ray-Jones

affection for at least one or two seaside resorts; and when they get within sight of a pier or a promenade revert quite naturally to the pleasures and pastimes of childhood, and behave much as the Edwardian, Victorian or even Regency visitor to the seaside did before them.

> – Ah, still the same, the same
> As it was last year and the year before –
> But rather more expensive, now, of course

wrote John Betjeman in his poem *Beside the Seaside* which was published in the late 1940s. The lines still apply, and perhaps might be borrowed to finish this book.

Bibliography

Adburgham, Alison *A Punch History of Manners and Modes 1840–1940*, Hutchinson, London 1961

Addison, William *English Spas*, Batsford, London 1951

Amory, Cleveland *The Last Resorts*, Harper Brothers, New York 1948

Ardagh, John *The New France*, Penguin Books, London 1970

Austen, Jane *Sanditon* in *Minor Works*, ed. R. W. Chapman, Oxford University Press, Oxford 1954

Ayton, Richard and Daniell, William *A Voyage Round Great Britain*, 8 vols., Longman, London 1814–25

Banham, Rayner *Los Angeles*, Penguin Press, London 1970

Beach, Rex (George Merrick) *The Miracle of Coral Gables*, Coral Gables, Florida 1926

Becker, Bernard *Holiday Haunts*, Remington, London 1884

Bede, Cuthbert (Rev. Edward Bradley) *Mattins and Muttons*, Sampson Low, London 1866

Best, Geoffrey *Mid-Victorian Britain 1851–1875*, Weidenfeld & Nicolson, London 1971

Betjeman, John *First and Last Loves*, John Murray, London 1952

Betjeman, John and Gray, S. J. *Victorian and Edwardian Brighton from Old Photographs*, Batsford, London 1972

Boussel, Patrice *Histoire des Vacances*, Berger-Levrault, Paris 1961

Brewster (Gordon), Margaret, Maria *Letters from Cannes and Nice*, Constable, Edinburgh 1857

Buxton, Elizabeth Ellen *Ellen Buxton's Journal 1860–1864*, ed. Ellen R. C. Creighton, Geoffrey Bles, London 1967

Cable, Mary 'The Marble Cottages' in *Horizon*, vol. VII, no. 4, 1965

Calder-Marshall, Arthur *Wish you Were Here – The Art of Donald McGill*, Hutchinson, London 1952

Carline, Richard *Pictures in the Post*, Gordon Fraser, London 1959

Chesney, Kellow *Victorian Underworld*, M. T. Smith, London 1970

Clarke, Charles Allen *The Story of Blackpool*, Palatine Books, Blackpool 1923

Cook, Edwin and Olive 'Beside the Seaside' in *The Saturday Book*, vol. 12, Hutchinson 1952

Duff, David *Victoria Travels*, Frederick Muller, London 1970

Dulles, Foster Rhea *America Learns to Play*, D. Appleton-Century, New York 1940

Eyre, Kathleen *Seven Golden Miles*, Weaver & Youles, Lytham St Annes 1961

Eyre, Kathleen *Bygone Blackpool*, Hendon Publishing Co., Nelson 1971

Fried, F. *A Pictorial History of the Carousel*, A. & S. Barnes, New York 1964

Frondeville, Guy de *Les Visiteurs de la Mer*, Le Centurion, Paris 1956

Gatty, Margaret *British Seaweeds*, London 1863

George, Mary Dorothy *Hogarth to Cruikshank, Social Change in Graphic Satire*, Allen Lane, Penguin Press, London 1967

Gilbert, E. W. *Brighton, Old Ocean's Bauble*, Methuen, London 1954

Girouard, Mark 'Cromer, Norfolk' in *Country Life*, 19 and 26 August 1971

Godden, Geoffrey A. *The Illustrated Guide to Lowestoft Porcelain*, Herbert Jenkins, London 1962

Goffin, J. R. 'Goss China' in *Country Life*, 30 September and 6 October 1971

Gosse, Edmund *Father and Son*, Heinemann, London 1907

Granville, A. B. *Spas of England and Principal Sea-Bathing Places*, 3 vols., 1841, reprinted with an introduction by Geoffrey Martin, Adams & Dart, London 1971

Graves, Charles *Royal Riviera*, Heinemann, London 1951

Heckstall-Smith, Anthony   *Sacred Cowes,*
   Anthony Blond, London 1965

Hern, Anthony   *The Seaside Holiday,* Cresset
   Press, London 1967

Hillier, Bevis   *Art Deco,* Studio Vista, London and
   Dutton, New York 1968

Holt, Tonie and Valmai   *Picture Postcards of the
   Golden Age,* MacGibbon & Kee, London 1971

Howe, Bea   *Antiques from the Victorian Home,*
   Batsford, London 1973

Howe, Bea   'A Hobby for Victorian Ladies,
   Seawood Collecting' in *Country Life,*
   20 February 1958

James, Henry   'An International Episode' in
   The Complete Tales, vol. 4, 1876–1882, ed. Leon
   Edel, Rupert Hart-Davis, London 1964

Jefferies, John Richard   *The Open Air,* Chatto &
   Windus, London 1885

Johnson, Alva   *The Incredible Mizners,* Rupert
   Hart-Davis, London 1953

Jones, Barbara   *The Unsophisticated Arts,*
   Architectural Press, London 1951

Kingsley, Charles   *Glaucus,* Macmillan,
   Cambridge 1855

Lancaster, Osbert   *Progress at Pelvis Bay,*
   John Murray, London 1936

Laver, James   *Victorian Vista,* Hulton Press,
   London 1954

Laver, James   *Edwardian Promenade,*
   Edward Hulton, London 1958

Laver, James   *Between the Wars,* Vista Books,
   London 1961

Lichten, Frances   *Decorative Arts of Victoria's
   Era,* Scribner, New York 1950

Lindley, Kenneth   *Seaside Architecture,* Hugh
   Evelyn, London 1973

Lock, F. P.   'Jane Austen and the Seaside' in
   Country Life Annual, 1972

Lyon, Peter   'The Master Showman of Coney
   Island' in *American Heritage,* June 1958

Manning-Sanders, Ruth   *Seaside England,*
   Batsford, London 1951

Manwaring Baines, J.   *Historic Hastings,* Parsons,
   Hastings 1955

Marsden, Christopher   *The English at the Seaside,*
   Collins, London 1947

Maxwell, Constantia   *The English Traveller in
   France 1698–1815,* Routledge, London 1932

Mayer, Grace M.   *Once Upon a City,* Macmillan,
   New York 1958

McCollough, David   'Oak Bluffs' in *American
   Heritage,* October 1967

Musgrave, Clifford   *Life in Brighton,* Faber,
   London 1970

Myerscough, John   *The Victorian Development
   of the Seaside Holiday Industry* (conference
   report of the Victorian Society), 1967

North, Rex   *The Butlin Story,* Jarrolds, London
   1962

Pakenham, Simona   *Sixty Miles from England,
   The English in Dieppe 1814–1914,* Macmillan,
   London 1967

Pimlott, J. A. R.   *The Englishman's Holiday,*
   Faber, London 1947

Pinto, Edward and Eva   *Tunbridge and Scottish
   Souvenir Woodware,* Bell, London 1970

Plumb, J. H.   *Men and Places,* Cresset Press,
   London 1963

Rose, Clarkson   *Beside the Seaside,* Museum Press,
   London 1960

Rowsome, F.   *Trolley Car Treasury,*
   McGraw-Hill, New York 1956

Scott, George Ryley   *The Story of Baths and
   Bathing,* Werner Laurie, London 1939

Seaton, Meg   *Sweets,* Whitechapel Art Gallery,
   London 1973

Silver, Nathan   *Lost New York,* Houghton
   Mifflin, New York 1967

Sitwell, Osbert and Barton, Margaret   *Brighton,*
   Faber, London 1935

Stokes, H. G.   *The English Seaside,* Sylvan Press,
   London 1947

Surtees, R. S.   *Plain or Ringlets,* London 1860

Swan, R. G.   'Naturalists and Beachcombers –
   The Victorian Mania for the Seashore' in
   Country Life, 2 May 1968

Thackeray, W. M.   *The Newcomes,* London 1854

Tindall, George B.   'The Bubble in the Sun' in
   American Heritage, August 1965

Tomkins, Calvin   *Living Well is the Best Revenge,*
   Deutsch, London 1973; as *Villa America,*
   Viking Press, New York 1971

Trollope, Frances   *Domestic Manners of the
   Americans,* 1832; reprinted, Alfred A. Knopf,
   New York 1949

Wecter, Dixon   *The Saga of American Society,*
   Scribner, New York 1970

Weightman, J. G.   'A View of the Côte d'Azur' in
   Encounter, October 1959

Weightman, J. G.   'The Solar Revolution' in
   Encounter, December 1970

Wilson, Harold F.   *The Story of the Jersey Shore,*
   The New Jersey Historical Series, D. Van
   Nostrand, Princeton 1964

Wolverhampton Museum and Art Gallery
   A Present From . . . (catalogue of an exhibition of
   seaside souvenirs), Wolverhampton 1972

Illustration sources

The references are to page numbers.

Miss Amy Bailey 137, 157   Barnaby's Picture Library 196   B. T. Batsford Ltd 186–7   Mr H. Beresford-Bourke 119, 130, 134, 140, 148   Blackpool Public Library 171   Brighton Museum and Art Gallery 36, 38, 47   Brighton Public Library 24, 50, 113, 181 (top)   Bristol Museum and Art Gallery 77   British Museum, London 21 30, 33, 40–1, 49, 58   Butlins Ltd 190   Crown Publishers Inc 62, 66 (taken from *The Wood Engravings* of Winslow Homer, ed. Barbara Gelman, published 1969)   Mr Michael Davies 143   Dover Publications Inc 163 (taken from *The Gibson Girl and her America*, published 1969)   Duke's County Historical Society 64, 159   Mary Evans Picture Library 127, 132   Fox Photos 183   French Government Tourist Office 194   Mr Frederick Fried 165 (top) (taken from *A Picture History of the Carousel*)   Glasgow Art Gallery and Museum 59   (Burrell Collection) Mr J. S. Gray 73, 105   Hastings Public Library 124   The Historical Association of Southern Florida 184   *The Illustrated London News* 146, 150   Miss Barbara Jones 97, 101 (lower), 112, 125, 137, 139   Library of Congress, Washington 110, 165 (lower), 167, 168   Raymond Mander and Joe Mitchenson Theatre Collection 122   Mansell Collection 69, 118   Clare Martin, Peter Jones and Trevor Denning 200   Collection of Mr and Mrs Paul Mellon 22, 153 (top)   Miami Beach Tourist Office 198   Museo del Prado, Madrid 152   Museum of British Transport 173 (top)   Museum of the City of New York 160 (Byron Collection), 169   Music for Pleasure 199 (LP Sleeve)

National Gallery London 153 (lower)   City of Norwich Museums 28 (top)   Mr Michael Palmer and Mr Michael Simpkin 138   Mr Ronald Pearsall 84   Preservation Society of Newport County 162   Proprietors of *Punch* 74, 82, 88, 98, 182   Radio Times Hulton Picture Library title page, 6, 12, 26, 53, 60, 76, 102, 106, 115, 117   © Anna Ray-Jones 201   Royal Institute of British Architects, Drawings Collection 35   Mr Morton Sands 120 (below)   Scarborough Museum and Art Gallery (Laughton Collection) 15   Science Museum, London 109   Mr Robert Scott 91, 140, 189, 191   Mrs F. Smith 95   Mr R. L. Smith 128–9   © SPADEM 177   Stoke on Trent City Museum and Art Gallery 25   The Sutcliffe Gallery, Whitby 123   Syndication International 135, 199 (photo only)   Tate Gallery, London 68, 92–3   Victoria and Albert Museum, London 45, 104   Verkerke Reprodukties N.V. 156   Mrs Beryl Vosburgh 192 (top)   The White House Collection of Art 120 (top)   Wolverhampton Art Gallery and Museums 28 (lower)

The photographs on the following pages were taken by:

Michael Blaker and M. and A. Keniger 192 (lower four)   A. C. Cooper 79   Deste Photography 173 (top)   Frank Greaves 196   Herbert of Weymouth 95   Eric de Maré 36   Tony Ray-Jones 201   John Webb 68

Index

Numbers in italics refer to illustration pages